Intentional Leadership

Intentional Leadership: Becoming a Trustworthy Leader clearly explains the ways leaders can build trust in three stages of their career: as an individual contributor, as a team member, and as a leader of an organization.

Through profiling a trustworthy leader, Bob Lintz, and his career at General Motors, this text illustrates how leaders can be intentional in leading themselves, their teams, and their organizations by building the ROCC of Trust (be reliable, open and honest, competent, and compassionate). The authors also feature other authentic leaders to demonstrate how to build trust along your leadership journey. Some noteworthy differences from this book's first edition include:

- Revised from the first edition with more than 80% new material to help leaders at all ages and all stages build trust and move from an individual contributor to an organizational leader.
- Each chapter is structured around the career of Bob Lintz, who successfully turned around a failing GM plant in the suburb of Cleveland. He now serves The Cleveland Clinic's Board of Trustees where he is applying the lessons learned from this turnaround.
- Each chapter also contains the experience and wisdom of other trustworthy leaders from a variety of backgrounds, ethnicities, and economic sectors; this will inspire other leaders to build trust intentionally and authentically.
- An accessible and informative tone, with a focus on research and anecdotes, to create a cohesive guidebook for leaders.

Intentional Leadership is suitable for new as well as experienced leaders who want to learn more about how to build trust with employees and other stakeholders, and who want to be intentional in the way they lead others.

Karen E. Mishra, Ph.D., serves as an Associate Professor of Business at Campbell University's Lundy-Fetterman School of Business. She is a Gallup Certified Strengths coach and helps her students and clients understand, appreciate, and make the most of their strengths in their careers. Dr Mishra has held positions teaching marketing and leadership at numerous universities including but not limited to North Carolina State University, East Carolina University, Meredith College, and Michigan State University.

Aneil K. Mishra, Ph.D., is the Dean of the School of Management at University of Michigan-Flint. He previously served as the Thomas D. Arthur Distinguished Professor of Leadership at East Carolina University. Prior to that, he was Associate Dean of Academic Affairs at North Carolina Central University in Durham, NC.

Leadership: Research and Practice Series

Series Editor: Ronald E. Riggio
Henry R. Kravis Professor of Leadership and Organizational Psychology
Kravis Leadership Institute, Claremont McKenna College

In Memoriam
Georgia Sorenson (1947–2020), Founding Editor

Becoming a Leader
Nine Elements of Leadership Mastery
Al Bolea and Leanne Atwater

Leadership Across Boundaries
A Passage to Aporia
Nathan Harter

A Theory of Environmental Leadership
Leading for the Earth
Mark Manolopoulos

Handbook of International and Cross-Cultural Leadership Research Processes
Perspectives, Practice, Instruction
Edited by Yulia Tolstikov-Mast, Franziska Bieri, and Jennie L. Walker

Deepening the Leadership Journey
Nine Elements of Leadership Mastery
Al Bolea and Leanne Atwater

Donald Trump in Historical Perspective
Dead Precedents
Edited by Michael Harvey

Intentional Leadership
Becoming a Trustworthy Leader
Karen E. Mishra and Aneil K. Mishra

For more information about this series, please visit: www.routledge.com/
Leadership-Research-and-Practice/book-series/leadership

Intentional Leadership

BECOMING A TRUSTWORTHY LEADER

Second Edition

Karen E. Mishra and Aneil K. Mishra

Routledge
Taylor & Francis Group

NEW YORK AND LONDON

Cover image: © Getty Images

Second edition published 2023
by Routledge
605 Third Avenue, New York, NY 10158

and by Routledge
4 Park Square, Milton Park, Abingdon, Oxon, OX14 4RN

Routledge is an imprint of the Taylor & Francis Group, an informa business

© 2023 Karen E. Mishra and Aneil K. Mishra

First edition published by Routledge 2013

Library of Congress Cataloging-in-Publication Data
Names: Mishra, Karen E., author. | Mishra, Aneil, author.
Title: Intentional leadership: becoming a trustworthy leader/Karen E.
Mishra and Aneil K. Mishra.
Other titles: Becoming a trustworth leader
Description: Second edition. | New York, NY: Routledge, 2022. | Series:
Leadership: research and practice | Includes bibliographical
references and index. |
Identifiers: LCCN 2022012854 (print) | LCCN 2022012855 (ebook) |
ISBN 9780367421472 (hardback) | ISBN 9780367421458 (paperback) |
ISBN 9780367822170 (ebook)
Subjects: LCSH: Leadership. | Trust.
Classification: LCC HD57.7. M575 2022 (print) | LCC HD57.7 (ebook) |
DDC 658.4/092–dc23/eng/20220321
LC record available at https://lccn.loc.gov/2022012854
LC ebook record available at https://lccn.loc.gov/2022012855

ISBN: 978-0-367-42147-2 (hbk)
ISBN: 978-0-367-42145-8 (pbk)
ISBN: 978-0-367-82217-0 (ebk)

DOI: 10.4324/9780367822170

Typeset in Palatino
by KnowledgeWorks Global Ltd.

To the Glory of the Lord

and

In memory of our sister Dr. Lisa Lynne Repaskey an empathic, authentic, courageous, and humble leader who made such a positive difference in the lives of so many, and who was taken before her time.

CONTENTS

x   Contents

ACKNOWLEDGMENTS

This book would not be possible without the continuing example of Bob Lintz, former General Motors Parma plant manager and current trustee of the Cleveland Clinic. We are grateful to Bob for his continuing friendship, mentorship, and inspiring example of a trustworthy leader.

We are grateful to all of the leaders who contributed their insights and ideas, whom we quote with their permission throughout the book.

We are grateful to Tom Arthur for his generous support of East Carolina University in the form of the Tom Arthur Distinguished Professor of Leadership that has supported Aneil's professorship for his seven years in the College of Business at East Carolina University. Tom's example as a trustworthy leader and philanthropist are an inspiration to us as well.

We are grateful to Campbell University for the summer research grant that allowed us to make time to finish the writing of this book during the summer of 2021.

We thank Christina Peterides at Last Glance for her superb copyediting.

Last, but not least, we are grateful to our two adult children Maggie and Jack who are our greatest source of love and encouragement. We are so proud of the young leaders they have become.

SERIES FOREWORD

We are in a perilous age where trust in institutions, and in those who lead them, is at a low. Traditional approaches to leadership focus on leader power, decisiveness, and control. Yet, leadership is, at its heart, about relationships. And, without trust, relationships can wither and die. So, it is very important that this book, *Intentional Leadership: Becoming a Trustworthy Leader*, arrive at this point in history in order to focus our attention on the important role of trust in the leader-follower relationship.

How do leaders build trust? Drs. Karen and Aneil Mishra have created a handbook that will guide leaders through that process. Drawing on theories and research on exemplary leadership, they show us the elements of great leadership—empathy, authenticity, courage, humility—qualities that until recent years went unnoticed and understudied in the leadership literature.

Through anecdotes about effective and exemplary leaders (and you will "meet" many of them), and with straightforward strategies for developing leadership and creating and maintaining more effective teams, the Mishras have written an easy-to-use guide that will help any leader become better.

It has been exciting to have the Mishras featured in our book series. In this volume, and in their previous book, *Becoming a Trustworthy Leader*, the authors are able to rely on basic research in effective leadership and teamwork and provide practical lessons for leaders at all stages of their careers. These represent what this book series is all about: *Leadership: Research and Practice*.

Ronald E. Riggio, Ph.D.
Henry R. Kravis Professor of Leadership and Organizational Psychology
Kravis Leadership Institute
Claremont McKenna College

INTRODUCTION

BOB LINTZ IS THE BEST BOSS WE NEVER HAD

One of the key inspirations for this book, and all our books on leadership, has been Bob Lintz. This is quite an admission for two Michigan Wolverines to make about a Michigan State Spartan. Bob was the General Motors (GM) Company plant manager who led a turnaround of the company's transmission and metal-stamping plant in Parma, Ohio, a suburb of Cleveland. Bob's leadership of GM's three-million square foot Metal Fabrication Division (known as the Parma Metal Center) from the mid-1970s until the end of the 1990s resulted in saving several thousand automotive industry jobs, achieving several hundreds of millions of dollars in cumulative cost savings, as well as ongoing savings in the tens of millions of dollars, and creating one of the world's best metal fabricating operations today in terms of quality, productivity, and innovative labor-management practices.

In leading Parma for 25 years, from 1973 to 1999, Bob not only sacrificed personally, in terms of time away from his family, but also professionally, by regularly turning down promotions in order to create the culture change that took many years first to achieve and then to cement. One example of this culture change is that Bob's initial successor, one of his former subordinates who had become a plant manager elsewhere within GM, was removed after only six months because he attempted to return to a command-and-control, hierarchical form of management. The next replacement, also a former lieutenant of Bob's, continued with Bob's trust- and empowerment-based form of leadership, which has continued to the present day.

When Aneil took over as the doctoral research assistant for an automotive research study at the University of Michigan in 1990, he interviewed Bob as part of the final round of interviews for this project. As a way to build trust with Bob, Aneil brought the front and sports sections of the Sunday edition of *Ann Arbor News* following Michigan's horrific defeat by Bob's beloved Michigan State University (MSU) Spartans, at 28–27. Michigan was ranked number one in the country at the time, and MSU ruined the Wolverines' chances for the national title by defeating them. Bob was quite impressed that Aneil would be so humble as to as provide this gift to him, since Wolverines fans were assumed by Spartans to be some of the most arrogant people in the country. This was the beginning of a deep, trust-based friendship. Following their first meeting, the topic of trust was the highlight of any discussion. What

DOI: 10.4324/9780367822170-1

began as a result of that initial conversation was a relationship that would span three decades. These stories about Bob and his trustworthy leadership have provided us with inspiration about how to be better leaders and teammates, and we hope that they will inspire you as well.

WHY TRUST MATTERS FOR LEADERSHIP

Throughout this book, using our ROCC of Trust model, we will discuss how leaders build trust to determine whether leaders are reliable, open/honest, competent, and caring. (The ROCC of Trust is covered in detail in Chapter 3.) When we ask students and executives about the best boss they ever had, they always tell us that this person showed that they cared about them and their career. It is not that this boss was an expert in their field or showed up on time to work every day (competent or reliable), but that they were transparent with them and showed that they were concerned about their welfare (caring and openness). We will explore the four dimensions of trustworthy leadership further together with what we have learned from Bob's example in order to help you be *intentional* in your pursuit to be the trustworthy leader you admire in your best boss.

This book is for individuals who aspire to become trustworthy, transformative leaders. Our research that forms the foundation for this book initially began during a crisis—namely, the crisis faced by the North American automotive industry in the late 1980s and early 1990s. We both worked for GM (though not for Bob) before beginning our graduate programs: an MBA for Karen and a Ph.D. in business for Aneil, both at the University of Michigan Ross School of Business. After teaching leadership and serving in leadership positions ourselves, we believe that anyone can improve their own leadership behaviors and styles, if they are intentional about it.

You will meet new leaders here that you have not heard of before. There is a reason for this. We like to profile leaders who can teach us all something through their actions and outcomes about how to be a more trusted leader. We chose them based on our up-front observations of their leadership examples and results. In addition, they represent:

- a more diverse group of people than you might normally read about
- leaders with a wide-ranging set of perspectives
- leaders who have taken atypical career paths
- leaders who are quiet in the way they engage and serve others.

YOUR LEADERSHIP JOURNEY

As you begin your leadership journey, you will establish yourself as a leader even before you take on official leadership duties. The way you carry yourself, turn in assignments, show up to work, and contribute to your team all tell your manager what kind of leader you will be in the future.

In the beginning, your reliability and competence will be heavily scrutinized, because those two traits are most easily identified and quickly noticed by others. This is important to understand because you can control how responsive you are—for example, to emails (reliability)—or how attentive you are to turning in quality work (competence). In addition, if you feel you need to improve in these areas, they are relatively easily developed.

Later, as you move into higher levels of leadership, your ability to be open and honest, along with the way you show that you care for others, will more clearly illustrate your leadership ability. While competence might get you promoted to team leader, openness and caring will get you promoted to organizational leader. Organizations want to know that their leader is concerned about others as well, not just themselves. Increasing these two parts of the ROCC of Trust, moreover, takes much more effort, but that also makes them much more valuable than either reliability or competence.

You will see your role as a leader evolve over time as well and realize the importance of middle managers in preserving culture and maintaining the trust of employees. Organizational leaders rely on middle managers to communicate strategies and objectives to lower-level employees, and they in turn rely on middle managers to show them they have their best interests at heart by developing them and guiding their careers. In this way, the organizational psychologist Rensis Likert labeled them "linking pins" due to their key role in facilitating work relationships up and down the organization.[1] Figure 0.1 illustrates these three levels of leadership (Mishra & Mishra, 2022). We will

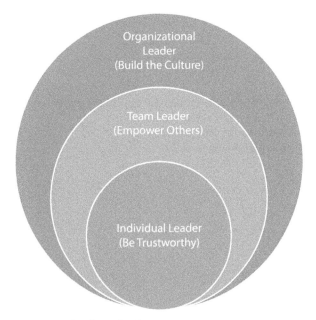

Figure 0.1 The Three Levels of Leadership

also describe how training and developing middle managers will help both your employees and your organization.

Finally, we will explore the importance of organizational leaders building a culture of trust, which includes emphasizing the value of human capital. This involves promoting positive leadership and selflessness, focusing on building trust rather than undermining it, and retaining your best employees—those who have valuable experience, skills, and strengths.

THE STATE OF LEADERSHIP

A recent study by DDI, a global consulting firm,[2] illustrates the challenges and opportunities for intentional leaders to start building the next generation of trustworthy leaders. In this study, 50% of chief executive officers (CEO) said that developing the next generation of talent is a key concern of theirs, especially because of employee burnout, disengagement, and mass resignations taking place during the COVID-19 pandemic. Both CEOs and chief human resources officers (CHRO) see that aspiring leaders are missing out on key skills such as empathy, communication, coaching, and building partnerships. Aspiring leaders also see that they are missing out on opportunities to learn these skills and seek both in-person and virtual training programs to improve their emotional intelligence, or EQ, communication, and leadership skills. If companies do not address this disconnect, they risk losing 86% of their high-potential employees.[3]

Our goal for this book is to provide you with stories and examples that will help you build your own leadership potential as an individual contributor, team leader, and one who ultimately builds a culture of trust.

Notes

1. Likert, R. (1981). System 4: A resource for improving public administration. *Public Administration Review*, 41(6), 674–678.
2. https://www.ddiworld.com/ (2021)
3. https://www.ddiworld.com/ (2021)

PART I

LEADING YOURSELF (BE TRUSTWORTHY)

1 LEADERSHIP IS INTENTIONAL

In Bob's first month at General Motors (GM), the general superintendent of the Chevrolet plant at which Bob worked, and someone several levels higher than Bob, came up and introduced himself saying, "Hey, aren't you Robert Lintz? Glad to have you here." Bob certainly knew who Mr. Salgot was, even though he had never personally met him. He was a very dignified, distinguished-looking individual. He usually dressed in a three-piece suit and wore a tiepin. Frank then asked Bob: "Well, Robert, if there is anything I could ever do for you, just let me know." Bob thought that was great of him to ask this. However, because nobody but Bob's parents called him Robert, without thinking he spat out, "Mr. Salgot, I'd just as soon be called Bob if that's okay with you." As Bob said to us, "He looked me in the eye and said, 'Yes, Robert,'" before adding, "I certainly knew my place in the pecking order. Frank was way up there and I was way down here."

Excellent leaders are *intentional*. By that, we mean that they have a deliberate purpose in their lives to help transform their teams and their organizations into being their very best. In addition, they make intentional decisions in how they lead, not just to be a leader in name only. When people truly want to be excellent leaders, they need to take the necessary steps. Such steps include identifying their strengths and weaknesses, continually developing those strengths, and collaborating with others in ways that maximize their collective strengths and offset any weaknesses. Finally, trustworthy leaders enlarge their purpose to develop a hopeful vision of the future that enriches their communities and society at large.

Too many people want to be leaders but are neither proactive nor deliberative about it. Others are thrust into leadership positions without any preparation. The first group often never end up really leading, and the latter underperform or fail as leaders. As a result, teams and organizations also fail.

Lest readers think that we are describing superhumans, we argue just the opposite. Ordinary people have overcome seemingly huge difficulties or dispiriting setbacks to build incredible organizations, because they have done so by embracing paradoxes.[1] They are both courageous and humble, convinced of their uniqueness yet doggedly collaborative, endlessly optimistic while relentlessly realistic. We also argue that such leaders do so by building trust in four key ways, which we call the ROCC of Trust: Reliability, Openness/ Honesty, Competence, and Caring. By doing so, these leaders inspire those teams and organizations in ways that other leaders, however capable, cannot.

DOI: 10.4324/9780367822170-3

Building such trust allows followers to believe that these leaders have both the capabilities and proper intentions to lead them past uncertainty and ambiguity, doubt, and despair. They pool scarce human material and financial resources, which are critical for innovating past their present circumstances. Mike Gannon, one of our former GM supervisors, shared with us how he built his leadership experience:

> Beginning in elementary school, and continuing through my college years, I sought out and was elected to numerous student government and Boy Scout leadership positions.

There are literally thousands of studies on leadership, and probably as many books. The number of definitions of leaders and leadership reflects this vast work and incorporates such elements as personality traits, skills, patterns of behavior, and contexts (e.g., for-profit, not-for-profit, military, government) to name a few. One classic definition, and one of our favorites, is by leadership scholar John Kotter:

> Management is a set of processes that can keep a complicated system of people and technology running smoothly. Leadership is a set of processes that creates organizations in the first place or adapts them to significantly changing circumstances. Leadership defines what the future should look like, aligns people with that vision, and inspires them to make it happen despite the circumstances.[2]

Given that we are focusing on trustworthy leadership, we will use and build on the definition of positive leadership by Dr. Kim Cameron, a University of Michigan Ross School of Business emeritus professor and a mentor to both of us:

> Positive leadership refers to an emphasis on what elevates individuals and organizations (in addition to what challenges them), what goes right in organizations (in addition to what goes wrong), what is life-giving (in addition to what is problematic or life-depleting), what is experienced as good (in addition to what is objectionable), what is extraordinary (in addition to what is merely effective), and what is inspiring (in addition to what is difficult or arduous). Positive leadership means promoting outcomes such as thriving at work, interpersonal flourishing, virtuous behaviors, positive emotions, and energizing networks. The focus is primarily on the role of positive leaders in enabling positively deviant performance.[3]

One recent study found that leaders often emerge as a result of who talks the most in an organization.[4] This should help alert more introverted executives to speak up when an important topic is on the agenda, so that others will view you as a leader as well. It should also alert extroverted leaders to the fact that there are likely many quiet leaders among them who may have been overlooked. Another study showed that leaders may emerge as a result of the context of where they work and the followers who may or may not identify them as leaders.[5] This study demonstrates that followers can develop their leadership capability when encouraged to do so. Prompting employees to be more self-aware of their innate leadership abilities can help them see how they can become future leaders of their organization through their own leadership development.

THE IMPORTANCE OF TRUST

This book will emphasize the importance of leaders building trust with others if they want to achieve lasting, positive changes within their teams and organizations. We will be discussing both trustworthiness, or the attributes that motivate others to trust someone, and trust building—the actions leaders take to create a culture of trust, whether through behaviors they personally demonstrate or the practices, processes, and systems they help put into place that also foster trust but which are not dependent on an individual leader. As our friend and entrepreneurial leader in the energy sector, Jenny Meyer noted:

> In each of my roles, I took on more than necessary. It was important to have autonomy. The more trust I earned from my bosses, the more freedom I had to make decisions and build relationships.

One way we build trust with others is to learn their name. One study of college students found that they were more invested in a course and felt more valued when the professor knew their name.[6] The students also indicated that they would feel more comfortable talking with the professor about the course, or asking questions. This clearly demonstrates that being known by others helps us feel valued and included, which results in our being engaged and invested. There are many studies which demonstrate that engaged employees have a higher degree of trust in their manager,[7] so this is one good reason to know and use your employees' (or colleagues') names.

GM was our first "laboratory" where we both learned about leadership and followership—both the excellent and the not-so-good versions. When Karen was a co-op student at GM's Oldsmobile Division, her very first co-op supervisor asked, "Why are *you* here when my *wife* stays at home?" The message could not have been clearer: women belonged at home while men were the working professionals. After Aneil graduated from college, his first boss at Oldsmobile regularly threatened to "use his head as a pinata" whenever she was not perfectly satisfied with his work, or whenever an artificial deadline she had set for him loomed. Both of these experiences left us wondering if we were working in the right organization.

However, one of the very best bosses we each had was also a manager at Oldsmobile: Mike Gannon. Mike was Karen's supervisor when she was a co-op student in the Salaried Personnel Department—what is now known as human resources (HR). Mike also supervised Aneil when he was a summer intern before his senior year in college. Mike trusted each of us with very important projects that were often months long in scope and had high visibility within Oldsmobile. One of Mike's aims in mentoring us was to make us more effective contributors to his HR team.

For example, Aneil was given the responsibility of designing and implementing a survey of employees' attitudes towards quality and quality improvement. Successful completion of this project would, in turn, have a significant impact on the annual bonus for Oldsmobile's head of personnel, Mike's ultimate boss and one of the most powerful executives in the entire division. Mike trusted Karen with a project to create a new self-nomination system for employees to apply for internal jobs, rather than having to wait for their bosses to recommend them.

By empowering us, he demonstrated his trust in us. He also made us want to trust him more by making us feel protected whenever we made mistakes. During his summer internship, whenever Aneil made a noticeable mistake, Mike would always say, "*We* screwed up," rather than blaming Aneil. By feeling protected in this way, he encouraged us to innovate by being creative and taking reasonable risks.

Such a mistake happened during the first couple of weeks of Aneil's internship, when he mailed out a memo to 110 summer interns, with copies to each of their bosses, through the division's interoffice mailing system. The memo had been worded inappropriately (this was in 1983, before email was available).[8] Fixing the mistake required asking Oldsmobile secretaries located throughout the division's headquarter offices and various manufacturing plants to immediately physically remove each of the original 220 memos from 220 individual mailboxes and replace them with the revised memo Aneil wrote. When many of these secretaries' bosses called Personnel to complain about the extra work, Mike took the heat.

We have kept in touch with Mike to this very day since leaving GM. His career has taken him out of HRs into general management at the highest levels in manufacturing companies, which is rare enough. It has also taken him from working for GM to working for global firms, the first of which retained him as the sole executive they retained when they purchased some of GM's operations, something that is rarer still. When we think of leaders who empowered and encouraged their followers, we are proud to have had the opportunity to work for and learn from Mike Gannon. He described his motivation for being a leader this way:

> While I was growing up, my father was president of a community college. He was well known for driving innovation and for his far-reaching vision of what the college could become. It was hard not to notice how energized he was in striving for the vision of the college, but also how many others were inspired to help make the vision a reality.

I decided early on that the main reason I wanted to be a leader was to help inspire and lead people to achieve great things. It started out with small things, like being the best patrol in the troop, to making student government relevant, to becoming a world-class HR function, and ultimately to saving a company.

I think what Aneil and Karen may have sensed was that leadership for me has been more of a calling than a career goal. I have also found that when it is not really about me, and more about the good that can be accomplished, it is easier and more natural to embrace trust as a leadership style.

Questions to Consider

- What is your first memory of acting as a leader?
- When have you found yourself in a situation in which your values were at odds with the organization's?
- What choices have you made, like Mike, to become a leader and develop your leadership capability?

Notes

1. Cameron, K. S. (2008). Paradox in positive organizational change. *The Journal of Applied Behavioral Science, 44*(1), 7–24.
2. Kotter, J. P. (2012). *Leading change.* Harvard Business Review Press, p. 28.
3. Cameron, K. (2012). *Positive leadership: Strategies for extraordinary performance.* Berrett-Koehler Publishers.
4. Marchant, N. (2021, August 9). *People who speak more are more likely to considered to be leaders.* World Economic Forum. https://www.weforum.org/agenda/2021/08/leaders-talk-more-babble-hypothesis/
5. Bracht, E. M., Keng-Highberger, F. T., Avolio, B. J., & Huang, Y. (2021). Take a "selfie": Examining how leaders emerge from leader self-awareness, self-leadership, and self-efficacy. *Frontiers in Psychology, 12,* 653.
6. Cooper, K. M., Haney, B., Krieg, A., & Brownell, S. E. (2017). What's in a name? The importance of students perceiving that an instructor knows their names in a high-enrollment biology classroom. *CBELife Sciences Education, 16*(1), ar8.
7. Mishra, K., Boynton, L., & Mishra, A. (2014). Driving employee engagement: The expanded role of internal communications. *International Journal of Business Communication, 51*(2), 183–202.
8. As part of describing an upcoming picnic, Aneil had written, "BYOB." Several of the summer interns' bosses interpreted this as encouraging drinking (the drinking age was 18 back then, and everyone, or almost everyone, would have been of legal age). That was not Aneil's intention, since it was simply easier for everyone to bring whatever they wanted to drink, alcoholic or not, than to bring a bunch of sodas when there was a 10-cent deposit on each can or bottle. Fixing Aneil's mistake was as simple as reissuing the very same memo, word-for-word, but with "BYOB" spelled out as "bring your own beverage."

2

LEADERS **ARE** BORN
AND MADE

Bob began his career at General Motors (GM) in Flint, Michigan on Monday, June 17, 1963, eight days after graduating from MSU. After only eight hours of training, which focused on safety, he began supervising 35 hourly employees, represented by the United Auto Workers (UAW), the following day. He had been a summer intern in engineering the year before but had never worked on the factory floor. He was one of nine people hired into GM's new first-line supervisor program composed of brand-new college graduates. At age 22, he was about half the age of the youngest person he supervised. Most of his employees did not enjoy working at GM, and many of them did not even like each other. They had learned how to take advantage of their situation to do as little work as possible.

As one of these nine, first-line supervisor graduates, Bob was an anomaly. The people who worked for Bob were used to supervisors who had come up through the hourly employee ranks, bosses who had become "tough characters" through their bitter experiences, and whose preferred way to communicate was to creatively string together a set of swear words.

Once Bob's employees figured out that he was unlike the typical, up-from-the-ranks supervisors they had worked for their entire careers at GM; however, several of them started to give Bob some latitude when he made mistakes and even began helping him. One way that Bob had begun building trust with them from the outset was by taking a different approach. When he saw they were not doing their jobs, doing something they were not supposed to be doing, or violating the shop rules, instead of suspending them for five days—which was the typical response of other supervisors—he would talk to them instead. He would say, "Why are you doing that? You're here to do a job. You're getting paid. Why would you take advantage of the company that's paying you?" Their answers gave him insight into how they had been managed previously and allowed him to develop an alternative method. Bob's trust-based approach would ultimately create a transformational relationship between labor and management in what at the time was one of the most conflict-ridden and distrusting work environments in the United States.

If you have an early memory of being a leader, you might argue that leaders are born. After teaching leadership for decades, however, we also believe that leaders can be made. We argue that leaders have both inherent traits *and* learned abilities. Although some individuals are naturally more inclined to become leaders based on early life experiences and, yes, even genetics,[1] all

DOI: 10.4324/9780367822170-4

people have the capacity to *become* leaders if they first have the desire and second make the effort. Being an effective leader involves having certain traits with which a person might be born,[2] having the ability to learn specific skills and behaviors through developmental experiences, understanding one's personal orientation to learning (such as taking and analyzing the results of the Myers–Briggs Type Indicator, or MBTI), and receiving organizational support.[3,4,5,6] As our friend and ear, nose, and throat specialist Dr. Brent Senior of the University of North Carolina's School of Medicine put it:

> Leaders are never simply born. Vocal individuals may be born. Charismatic people may be born. But speaking and charisma only take the leader so far. Self-sacrificial, trustworthy leadership is something that goes against the natural bent of most individuals. It requires purposeful decision-making and introspection, and it can be made.

Empirical research bears out the argument that both nature and nurture shape leadership development. Based on a study using the Minnesota Twin Registry, Richard Arvey and his colleagues found that 30% of the leadership behaviors and the leadership roles that people occupy can be attributed to genetic factors, while the remaining 70% result from environmental factors.[7] In a subsequent study, these researchers found that environmental factors such as socioeconomic status, perceived parental support, and perceived conflict with parents all moderate the influence of genetic factors on whether or not a person occupies a leadership role.[8] A more recent twins' study was a little more conservative, finding that genetics contributed approximately one-quarter to leadership potential,[9] indicating that we are still able to become leaders due to other factors in our environment. "Leaders most likely arise from a combination of genetic predisposition as well as development through reactions to environmental factors."[10]

One of Aneil's former students, Juan Carolos Sanchez, remembered a time early in life when he considered himself a leader:

> I believe that the first time I acted as a leader was when I was seven or eight years old. My parents had just gotten divorced, things at home were unstable, and my younger sister who was five or six years old needed both support and guidance to deal with a mother who left home. Unbeknownst to me, my sister started both following my footsteps and relying on me for her mental well-being. She realized I was both her moral support and a positive role model she wanted to follow to keep growing in the right direction.

> It was possible for me to lead because of the mutual empathy and communication we had developed with one another. It could not have been possible had my sister not been open to my advice. By the same token, I always put myself in her shoes and sought to understand her position first before reaching any conclusion and/ or providing any insight or guidance to her.

Leaders' environments, especially early on, will also influence how and why they choose to lead. As Dr. Anitra Manning, one of Karen's former colleagues, stated:

> I saw a distributed leadership model in action as a child. My parents co-led their household without respect to gender. They jointly raised my sister and I with responsibilities divided based on convenience and capacity. My parents had been friends since the fifth grade and operated the house as friends committed to the spiritual growth and nurture of the other and their children. When my parents lived in Brooklyn, my mother had to leave the house at 4:30 a.m. so that she could pick us up from our church's private school at 4:00 p.m. As a result, my mother selected and ironed our clothes the night before and prepared huge meals on Sundays. My mother had to go to bed early and so my father did nightly bathtime, storytelling, and prayer rituals. He also prepared breakfast, helped us wash up, get dressed, drove us to school, and took us to church on Sundays. My mother picked us up, took us to the Brooklyn Public Library at Grand Army Plaza and the Brooklyn Children's Museum weekly, took us to art and enrichment classes, selected and ironed our clothes, and managed our hair grooming. My mother was active in the PTA and was highly visible at our schools. My mother also supported my father's desire to secure his master's degree (which he began when I was in high school). When we moved to Long Island, my father was responsible for taking us to the hair salon, cooking midweek meals, mowing the lawn, and taking out the trash.
>
> So that was the way the household worked. Both washed dishes, both cooked. So I was used to a shared leadership when I was at home with my parents. And I saw the same with my grandparents as well. My paternal grandparents shared in their responsibilities. Both of them could cook and did. Both of them cleaned the house. They were South Carolinian migrants and brought spirited and warm hospitality to everyone that visited with them. My grandfather managed the garden and backyard and my grandmother attended to the herbal and flower gardens. Because of the shared leadership and co-nurturing that was displayed in the lives of my parents, grandparents, and my extended paternal family, I expected that gender would not limit the success of women. I sincerely believed that. So much so, that when I saw my school district restricting the nomination of a woman principal in my high school at a board meeting, I went to the podium (with my mother and her friends cheering me on as I leaped from my seat in the Hempstead High School Little Theatre) and asked: if you have had 5 male principals, each failing to deliver…why not a woman?

My high school principal took note of this confident 14-year old. When that same 14-year old showed up to her office with a legal pad full of ideas to improve the academic and social climate of the school, that principal partnered with her so that each idea could become a reality.

Our friend Dr. Bruce Rubin, former chair of the pediatrics department at Virginia Commonwealth University and Richmond Children's Hospital, shared his perspective on leadership:

> I believe that leaders are born and made. I believe that the desire to lead is probably innate and appears in certain toddlers. I see young children who want to be leaders just as I see adults who embrace leadership opportunities. I believe that the ability to lead is learned over time and experience and it requires a passion and a desire to lead well. Desire to lead is not sufficient alone, but the willingness to be a learner and to continually strive to be the best leader that one can—this takes work.

Mike Gannon shared with us his ability to connect as a leader, despite his quiet nature:

> I recognized at a very early age that I had a burning desire to be a leader. I have a strong memory of my elementary school principal announcing an election for student council president. I remember thinking that I needed to be the president because I knew what should be done and how to make it happen. I was (and still am) shy and introverted, but my passion to be a leader was strong enough to overcome my fears, and I nominated myself as a candidate. My slogan, "I like Mike" was effective, and I ended up both winning the election and launching my leadership career.

Brooke Wilson, another leader we admire, along with her husband, Les, has been slowly growing her several franchises of Two Men and a Truck, International, a company which is based in Michigan. She and Les have expanded beyond North Carolina to include the Metro Atlanta area as well and shared with us her early recollections of her interest in leading:

> As a first-born child with a driven and successful business matriarch, I have always been driven to succeed. Because of my mother's professional ambitions, I relocated a lot. This likely contributed to the development of my people skills. The combination of desire to succeed and understanding the importance of influencing teams, united with an already-present "type A" personality trait, thereby positioned me as a leader.

Steve Fitzgerald, a former colleague of Aneil's, has had the opportunity to work with many other outstanding leaders and is self-aware of both his and their leadership abilities. He remembers some of his early evaluations by his teachers:

> As one teacher wrote, "Steve does not play well with others because he always has his opinion, and he wants to enforce that on others." But my kindergarten teacher said, "He is also one of the leaders in our classroom, because the kids generally come to see him for guidance as well as to coordinate their activities."

Leaders are critical to building trust in organizations, and when followers trust their leaders, those followers' actions and attitudes may benefit the organization significantly through better job performance, greater organizational commitment, higher job satisfaction, and lower intentions to quit.[11] Leaders who are trusted by their followers are also more easily able to effect change quickly in their organizations.[12] Of course, for change to take place in an organization, individuals must trust more than a single leader; they will distinguish between trusting a leader at the top of the organization versus trusting their own immediate bosses or other managers.[13,14,15]

Questions to Consider

- Do you have family members/teachers/mentors who are leaders? What did you learn from them?
- What leadership roles have you taken on in the past, and why did you do so?
- How does knowing you can grow as a leader encourage you to take on a new leadership role?

Notes

1. Johnson, A. M., Vernon, P. A., McCarthy, J. M., Molson, M., Harris, J. A., & Lang, K. L. (1998). Nature vs. nurture: Are leaders born or made? A behavior genetic investigation of leadership style. *Twin Research, 1*, 216–223.
2. Locke, E., & Kirkpatrick, S. (1999). *The essence of leadership: The four keys to leading successfully.* Lexington Books.
3. Gardner, J. W. (1993). *On leadership.* Free Press.
4. McCauley, C. D. (2001). Leader training and development. In S. J. Zaccaro, & R. J. Klimoski (Eds.), *The nature of organizational leadership* (pp. 347–383). Jossey-Bass.
5. Kouzes, J., & Posner, B. (2002). *The leadership challenge.* Jossey-Bass.
6. McCauley, C. D. (2001). Leader training and development. In S. J. Zaccaro, & R. J. Klimoski (Eds.), *The nature of organizational leadership* (pp. 347–383). Jossey-Bass.
7. Arvey, R. D., Rotundo, M., Johnson, W., Zhang, Z., & McGue, M. (2006). The determinants of leadership role occupancy: Genetic and personality factors. *The Leadership Quarterly, 17*, 1–20.

8. Zhang, Z., Ilies, R., & Arvey, R. (2009). Beyond genetic explanations for leadership: The moderating role of the social environment. *Organizational Behavior and Human Decision Processes, 110*, 118–128.
9. De Neve, J. E., Mikhaylov, S., Dawes, C. T. & Fowler, J. H. (2013). Born to Lead? A Twin Design and Genetic Association Study of Leadership Role Occupancy, *Leadership Quarterly, 24*(1), 45–60.
10. Boerma, M., Coyle, E. A., Dietrich, M. A., Dintzner, M. R., Drayton, S. J., Early, J. L., Edginton, A. N., Horlen, C. K., Kirkwood, C. K., Lin, A. Y.F., Rager, M. L., Shah-Manek, B., Welch, A. C., Toedter Williams, N., & Williams, N. T. (2017). Point/counterpoint: Are outstanding leaders born or made? *American Journal of Pharmaceutical Education, 81*(3), 1–5. (quote on p.5)
11. Dirks, K. T., & de Jong, B. (2021). Trust within the workplace: A review of two waves of research and a glimpse of the third. *Annual Review of Organizational Psychology and Organizational Behavior, 9*, 247–276.
12. McCallum, S., & O'Connell, D. (2008). Social capital and leadership development: Building stronger leadership skills through enhanced relationship skills. *Leadership & Organization Development Journal, 30*(2), 152–166.
13. Dirks, K. T., & Ferrin, D. L. (2002). Trust in leadership: Meta-analytic findings and implications for research and practice. *Journal of Applied Psychology, 87*(4), 611–628.
14. Gabarro, J. J. (1987). *The dynamics of taking charge.* Harvard Business School Press.
15. Spreitzer, G. M., & Mishra, A. K. (2002). To stay or to go: Voluntary survivor turnover following a downsizing, *Journal of Organizational Behavior, 23*(September), 707–729.

3 THE **ROCC** OF **TRUST**

In his first job at the Chevrolet plant in Flint, Bob had to learn a whole set of rules that seemed designed to put him in his place. One was about drinking coffee—which basically was that supervisors were not allowed to drink coffee. The logic was this: even though there were vending machines which dispensed coffee all over the plant, the only people on the shop floor who could drink coffee were the hourly employees during their scheduled breaks. First-line supervisors such as Bob were not given breaks, so they could not drink coffee. But, like most people, Bob needed some caffeine to get through his long days, so the trick was to grab a cup of coffee and then be as invisible as possible while drinking it. This meant ducking behind the vending machine or some other place to quickly gulp it down. He certainly could not drink it in front of his employees, because as a member of management, he officially did not take breaks, so he could not possibly have found time to get any coffee.

The management dress code also entailed a strict set of rules. First-line supervisors such as Bob wore white shirts and dark slacks. The next level of management wore their suit vests on top of the same shirts and dress pants. Only supervisors at levels above *that* could wear their suit jackets. One day Bob was sent home for not wearing a tie. Another time it was for wearing corduroys instead of dress slacks. Once, because his wife, Karen, had not done any laundry the night before, Bob came to work wearing a *blue* shirt; he got sent home to change and put on the required *white* shirt instead. In the world of General Motors (GM) in the 1960s, white-collar employees literally had to wear white shirts all the time.

Bob vowed that if he survived his first year as a supervisor and became a high-level manager himself one day, he would treat his employees very differently from the way he had been treated. To move up, however, he would first have to figure out how to drink coffee without getting caught by his bosses.

THE IMPORTANCE OF TRUST IN LEADERSHIP

In order to lead others, you will need to be able to influence them—in other words, get them to do what you want them to do. Influencing others, in turn, depends on a variety of factors. Some of these are about different kinds of power, including expertise; being respected, admired, or liked; and having a position of formal authority, among others. Another source of influence is being trusted.

DOI: 10.4324/9780367822170-5

Trust is presently so valuable because it is so rarely present. Indeed, a recent survey from PwC found that both leaders and employees value the role that trust plays in their organizations yet see how it works differently for each group.[1] For instance, leaders view their trust building in terms of how they communicate, whereas employees place a higher value on their leaders' accountability. An annual survey by Edelman finds that employee trust, and thus firm success, critically depends on employees having a positive work experience.[2]

Trust is more important for influencing others the greater the uncertainty, ambiguity, risk, or stakes that an organization faces. In addition, throughout the course of their careers, individuals may need to build trust with both leaders and subordinates (or other team members) at the same time. These are Likert's linking pins,[3] because they are the people who can build bridges of trust up and down the organization.

Most management and psychology researchers define trust as a willingness to be vulnerable to another person or party based on some positive expectations or beliefs regarding the other party's intentions or behavior.[4,5,6,7,8,9] Simply put, trust means you are willing to be vulnerable to others in the face of uncertainty. If you trust someone, you are more willing to become interdependent with that person, even though you cannot be sure everything will turn out well. There are times when you have no choice *but* to be vulnerable, such as when you are ill and rely on a doctor, a student and rely on a professor, or an employee and rely on a supervisor. Any time you have to depend on someone in some way which displays your own vulnerability, it heightens the awareness of the meaning of trust.

Phil Wilhelm, cybersecurity leader, defines trust as "when you are confident and happy putting your life in the hands of others. Your interactions with others and how you deal with them then form the basis for their expectations or beliefs, and thus the trust they have in you."[10] In our own three decades of research on trust within and across organizations, we have identified four distinct judgments or beliefs that are central to someone's trust in another, which comprise the trustworthiness of that other person.[11] These are Reliability, Openness, Competence, and Caring; what we call the ROCC of Trust.

The ROCC of Trust starts with Reliability. Trustworthiness in terms of reliability has been defined by other researchers as including consistency between one's words and actions, the predictability of action, or behavioral integrity.[12,13,14,15,16] Reliability is the first component of the ROCC of Trust because without it, others may not give us a second chance. Dennis Quaintance is the cofounder of Quaintance-Weaver Enterprises, and a regular guest speaker at our MBA classes. In 2007, he and his two partners built the hospitality industry's first LEED[17] Platinum-certified building, the Proximity Hotel, and Print Works Bistro. In 2017, he and his partners, one of whom is his wife, Nancy, sold their company to its employees through an employee stock ownership plan. They passed up on the higher valuation they would have received had they sold to another hospitality company.[18] In Quaintance's words:

> I do not believe in contrived ways of building trust. If you just talk the talk and walk the walk, make your own behavior consistent with the objectives and values of the organization, then folks will trust you. If you are a hypocrite, they will soon find that out as well. Do what you say you're going to do when you say you're going to do it.

The second part of the ROCC of Trust is Openness. Openness is a willingness to be honest and forthright in dealing with others. Several other scholars have also defined trustworthiness in terms of openness, transparency, or honesty.[19,20,21] In describing the Theory Z organizations, in which work relationships are characterized by mutual trust and influence, William Ouchi discussed trust extensively in terms of openness.[22] Leaders who are trusted are more effective in acquiring skills, retaining and attracting followers, promoting change and innovation,[23] and facilitating coordination among departments.[24] Openness thus embodies a willingness to listen to new ideas and perspectives. This mutual exchange of information creates a more trusting relationship. Being open also includes being evenhanded in sharing information or perspectives. Greater openness may entail risks, however. As our former pastor Jim Wenger of St. John Lutheran Church in Deshler, Ohio shares:

> One of my favorite books is *The Friendship Factor* by Alan Loy McGinnis. His strategy for building and sustaining friendships deals with disclosure; that is, sharing something about yourself. However, self-disclosure can be very risky. When we share something genuine about our true self, we risk being rejected, or the information being misused. I have long worked to develop small groups where people could share their interior life with a few other trusted people. When it works it is a very satisfying and fulfilling experience. When it doesn't it can be a disaster.

Competence is the third component of the ROCC of Trust. Competence includes the abilities, skills, and knowledge needed to achieve expected performance.[25] When we trust someone to be competent, we believe they have the abilities to perform their share of the workload.[26,27,28] Leaders are characterized by how much their followers trust them to make competent decisions that affect the group or organization.[29,30] Organizations spend a great deal of time and money on helping individuals become better leaders. The firm Training Industry estimated that $3.5 billion was spent by organizations around the globe in 2019 on leadership development.[31] A survey of 750 learning and development professionals reported that their firms spent on average $176 per employee on training and development in 2020, an increase over 2019, and approximately 25% of this was spent on leadership development.[32] Even if we are viewed as reliable and honest, people will not be willing to trust us unless we can do the job for which we were hired.

In certain circumstances, we use proxies for competence, such as a specific degree from a certain college. Still, direct experience with another person is a more convincing way to demonstrate competence. For instance, physicians almost always place their diplomas in their offices or examining rooms, but it is not until we spend time with and are treated by them that we determine whether we can truly trust them. Interestingly, competence is perhaps the easiest piece of the ROCC of Trust to improve. If we are not as competent as we desire in a certain skill or subject, we can always improve our knowledge or abilities through education or practice. Research has shown, however, that if we are not competent, others are likely to terminate their relationship with us.[33]

When we asked one automotive executive how his organization developed and maintained trust in the company, he stated:

> They've got to have some feeling that you're competent to lead them out of this mess. Because they may like you a lot, but if they feel you're a bumbling idiot they say, "Shit! We can't trust what this guy tells us. He's going to take us off the end of the cliff." I mean, they have to be confident that you're competent. They've got to have some feeling that you know what the hell you're talking about. When you go out there to tell them to do something, they've got to have some feeling that it will make a difference.[34]

Caring is the fourth part of the ROCC of Trust. At a minimum, when we trust someone to be caring or concerned about us, it means that we do not expect that person to take unfair advantage of us.[35,36] On the other side of the relationship, being trustworthy in this way means that we must be willing to take the time to understand another's needs or interests. It also means that we must place the interests of others at a level equal to or above our own. This is typically the last aspect of trust we learn about in others or that others know about us, because the other elements of the ROCC of Trust are easier to demonstrate in terms of their time commitment, the effort required, or both. Caring is valued so highly as an aspect of trust because it involves furthering others' interests and not just our own. As Bob told us many times, "You really have to be committed in your heart to doing what is right for the organization."

Empirical research has supported this four-dimensional categorization of trustworthiness.[37,38,39] One of the most highly cited articles in the field of management discussed three distinct dimensions of trustworthiness, two of which correspond to our Competence and Caring, with the third essentially combining Openness and Reliability.[40,41,42] Other empirical research has found strong support for five different dimensions of trustworthiness, four of which correspond directly to our four, with a fifth dimension differentiating integrity from predictability, or Reliability.[43]

Another of our other highly respected former supervisors, Anita Johnson, reflected on the ROCC of Trust in this way:

> In my opinion, openness and caring are important. They provide an opportunity for input perhaps not thought of before. Empathy and true listening build trust. Competence and reliability can be strengthened over time. Even for those not in agreement with a leader or a change management initiative, openness and caring may provide an opportunity for later buy-in due to the trust developed.

Questions to Consider

- How do you evaluate others when you are deciding if they are trustworthy? Which aspect of trust is more important to you?
- Of these four different ways to build trust, which one do you prefer to lead with yourself?
- Do you think one person can master all four aspects of trust at once, or must each be worked on at different times?

Notes

1. PWC. (2021, September 16). *Striking gaps between consumers', employees' and employers' definitions of "Trust" creates complex challenge for businesses, according to PwC survey*. https://www.pwc.com/us/en/press-releases/2021/complexity-of-trust.html
2. Edelman. (n.d.) *Employees now considered the most important group to companies' long-term success*. https://www.edelman.com/trust/2021-trust-barometer/spring-update/employees-now-considered
3. Likert, R. (1981). System 4: A resource for improving public administration. *Public Administration Review, 41*(6), 674–678.
4. Granovetter, M. (1985). Economic action and social structure: The problem of embeddedness. *American Journal of Sociology, 91*(3) (November), 481–510.
5. Lewis, J. D., & Weigert, A. (1985). Trust as a social reality. *Social Forces, 63*, 967–985.
6. Mishra, A. K. (1996). Organizational responses to crisis: The centrality of trust. In R. Kramer & T. Tyler (Eds.), *Trust in organizations* (pp. 261–287). Sage.
7. Mayer, R. C., Davis, J. H., & Schoorman, F. D. (1995). An integrative model of organizational trust. *Academy of Management Review, 20*, 709–734.
8. Sitkin, S. B., & Roth, N. L. (1993). Explaining the limited effectiveness of legalistic "remedies" for trust/distrust. *Organization Science, 4*, 367–392.
9. Rousseau, D. M., Sitkin, S. B., Burt, R. S., & Camerer, C. (1998). Not so different after all: A cross-discipline view of trust. *Academy of Management Review, 23*, 393–404.
10. Gabarro, J. (1987). *The dynamics of taking charge* (p. 104). Harvard Business School Press.
11. Consistent with most scholars, the trust someone has in another is based on 1) the trustor's propensity to trust in general, a personality trait, and 2) the trustworthiness of the person to be trusted.

12. McGregor, D. (1967). *The professional manager*. McGraw-Hill.
13. Gabarro, J. (1987). *The dynamics of taking charge* (p. 104). Harvard Business School Press.
14. Ouchi, William G. (1981). *Theory Z: How American business can meet the Japanese challenge*. Addison-Wesley.
15. Kirkpatrick, S., & Locke, E. (1991). Leadership: Do traits matter? *Academy of Management Executive, 5*(2), 48–60.
16. Simons, T. (2008). *The integrity dividend: Leading by the power of your word*. Jossey-Bass.
17. LEED (Leadership in Energy and Environmental Design) is a green building certification scheme run by the United States Green Building Council.
18. Burritt, C. (2017, November 3). *Dennis Quaintance's ESOP fable*. Business North Carolina. https://businessnc.com/dennis-quaintances-esop-fable/
19. Gabarro, J. (1987). *The dynamics of taking charge*. Harvard Business School Press.
20. Nanus, B. (1992). *Visionary leadership: Creating a compelling sense of direction for organizations*. Jossey-Bass.
21. Breuer, C., Huffmeier, J., Hibben, F., & Hertel, G. (2020). Trust in teams: A taxonomy of perceived trustworthiness factors and risk-taking behaviors in face-to-face and virtual teams. *Human Relations, 73*(1), 3–34.
    Bloom, P. (2016). *Against empathy: The case for rational compassion*. HarperCollins. Kindle edition, locations 164, 187.
22. Ouchi, William G. (1981). *Theory Z: How American business can meet the Japanese challenge*. Addison-Wesley.
23. Kilpatrick, S. A., & Locke, E. A. (1991). Leadership: Do traits matter? *Academy of Management Executive, 5*(2), 50–60.
24. Davis, S., & Lawrence, P. (1977). *Matrix*. Addison-Wesley.
25. Nooteboom, B. (2002). *Trust: Forms, foundations, functions, failures and figures*. Edward Elgar.
26. Mayer, R. C., Davis, J. H., & Schoorman, F. D. (1995). An integrative model of organizational trust. *Academy of Management Review, 20*, 709–734.
27. Szulanski, G., Cappetta, R., & Jensen, R. J. (2004). When and how trustworthiness matters: Knowledge transfer and the moderating effect of causal ambiguity. *Organization Science, 15*, 600–613.
28. Shapiro, D., Sheppard, B. B., & Cheraskin, L. (1992). Business on a handshake. *Negotiation Journal, 8*, 365–377.
29. Gabarro, J. (1987). *The dynamics of taking charge*. Harvard Business School Press.
30. Kilpatrick, S. A., & Locke, E. A. (1991). Leadership: Do traits matter? *Academy of Management Executive, 5*(2), 50–60.
31. Training Industry. (2019, March). *The State of the Leadership Training Market*.
32. Leinbach, M. (2021, May). 2021 Leadership development survey: The times they are a changing…, *Training*, 24–33. https://pubs.royle.com/publication/?m=20617&i=704776&p=26
33. Janowicz-Panjaitan, M., & Krishnan, R. (2009). Measures for dealing with competence and integrity violations of interorganizational trust at the corporate and operating levels of organizational hierarchy. *Journal of Management Studies, 46*(2), 245–268.
34. Mishra, A. K. (1996). Organizational responses to crisis: The centrality of trust. In R. Kramer & T. Tyler (Eds.), *Trust in organizations: Frontiers of theory and research* (p. 266). Thousand Oaks, CA: Sage.
35. McGregor, D. (1967). *The professional manager*. McGraw-Hill.

36. Cummings, L., & Bromiley, P. (1996). The organizational trust inventory (OTI): Development and validation. In R. Kramer, & T. Tyler (Eds.), *Trust in organizations: Frontiers of theory and research* (pp. 302–330). Sage.

37. Brockner, J., Spreitzer, G. M., Mishra, A. K., Hochwarter, W., Pepper, L., & Weinberg, J. (2004). Perceived control as an antidote to the negative effects of layoffs on survivors' organizational commitment and job performance. *Administrative Science Quarterly, 49*(1/March), 76–100.

38. Spreitzer, G. M., & Mishra, A. K. (2002). To stay or to go: voluntary survivor turnover following an organizational downsizing. *Journal of Organizational Behavior, 23*(6), 707–729.

39. Brahma, S. S. & Chakraborty, H. (2009). Assessment of construct validity of Mishra and Mishra's trust scale in the context of merger and acquisition in India. *Asian Journal of Management and Humanity Sciences, 4*(4), 200–225.

40. Mayer, R. C., Davis, J. H., & Schoorman, F. D. (1995). An integrative model of organizational trust. *Academy of Management Review, 20*(3), 709–734.

41. Schoorman, F. D., Mayer, R. C., & Davis, J. H. (2007). An integrative model of organizational trust: Past, present, and future. *The Academy of Management Review, 32*(2), 344–354.

42. Doney, P. M., & Cannon, J. P. (1997). An examination of the nature of trust in buyer–seller relationships. *Journal of Marketing, 61*(2), 35–51.

43. Breuer, C., Huffmeier, J., Hibben, F., & Hertel, G. (2020). Trust in teams: A taxonomy of perceived trustworthiness factors and risk-taking behaviors in face-to-face and virtual teams. *Human Relations, 73*(1), 3–34.

4 LEADING **WITH THE ROCC OF TRUST**

During the first few months working at GM, Bob would come home exhausted, not physically despite the long hours on his feet, but mentally. He really did not know if his bosses liked him because he seldom heard any praise. Instead, he received lot of criticism for things that they did not like. "To work in an environment like that was really stressful," Bob said. Almost every day he would complain to his wife, Karen, "Oh, my God, I can't believe I'm working in an environment like that." It was so different from how he had been brought up and how he had built friendships or related to others in college. Moreover, the top executives at GM Corporation had hired college graduates to be first-line supervisors to make a difference but Bob's management leaders at the Chevy plant didn't agree with the strategy. Bob told us:

> I'm trying to make a difference, but too many levels of manage-
> ment below those top executives, including many of my bosses,
> didn't want me to. They're the ones that made life the most diffi-
> cult. GM's top leadership either was not aware of this disconnect
> or chose not to become aware of it. The ultimate result was that six
> of the nine of us college graduates in this program quit in their first
> year on the job.

Becoming a trustworthy leader is about being intentional in how you lead and the way you build trust with others. It is thinking about your actions and inter-actions before you undertake them. Too many leaders think that they should be trusted just because they have the role or title of leader. The reality is that even without the official leader role or title, you can become a trusted leader through your intentional thinking, feeling, and behavior.

Moreover, rather than wait for others to trust us, as a leader we will sometimes find ourselves needing to trust first.[1] As a leader, you set the stage for your relationship with others (including your followers) by showing that you trust them. This intentional behavior shows that you, yourself, are trust-worthy, and your followers will then trust you. As president and cofounder of Rhino Foods Ted Castle told us:

> Trust is everything. Without a doubt, I trust people before they've
> earned or deserved it. I'm okay with that. Doesn't bother me at
> all. If somebody might violate my trust, well, I'm okay with that.

DOI: 10.4324/9780367822170-6

I'll just be more careful with that person next time. But I'm going to start from that spot. It starts with me, then the leadership team, then supervisors, then employees.

Regardless of your own trust-building preference for a given part of the ROCC of Trust, you also need to understand others' ROCC preferences and modify your approach as needed. It is like knowing how to speak each other's language. You will be able to communicate better once you understand each other better. Princeton alumnus John Rogers Jr. shared his experience of being trusted:

> Being a great teammate entails being a good listener and looking out for your teammates. At the same time, there's no substitute for hard work. It's also a really important thing to live up to the commitments that you make to each other. My co-CEO Melody Hobson would say that she always understood that whatever responsibilities she was given, she wanted to get them done, get them done well, and get them done early. It's in her DNA.

Previous research has shown that there are two underlying bases for assessing trustworthiness: cognitive (based on knowledge) and affective (based on emotion). Neither basis is more important than the other, and both are essential for judging whether someone else can be trusted. For instance, cognitive-based trust builds from our experience with others and having knowledge about a person's ability and/or competence, which tell us whether we can trust them in the future. Affective-based trust is based on the emotional connections we have with others, knowing that they care for us and value an ongoing relationship with us.[2]

The chart in Figure 4.1 depicts the four ways in which leaders initially prefer to build trust. All four parts of the ROCC of Trust are essential if one is to be viewed as a trustworthy leader. However, personality, experience, and other factors may influence which part of the ROCC of Trust a leader likes to demonstrate first. Of course, as one matures as a leader, it becomes easier to modify this preference as circumstances or followers dictate, but in novel or low-context situations with relatively few social cues or guidelines on to how to behave, leaders are more likely to revert to their preferred dimension.

The chart obviously simplifies trust building, as some leaders might like to combine two dimensions in their trust-building efforts, but we developed it so that you can begin to assess how you go about building trust with others more generally. Doing so will also help you understand where you might need to focus greater attention.[3] For example, Aneil typically likes to demonstrate his trustworthiness through Competence and Openness. He will share his background, experience, and facts about himself to others first, so that others can know who he is. On the other hand, Karen likes to build trust through Reliability and Caring. She shows others that they can trust her as she follows through on commitments and reaches out to others to show concern about

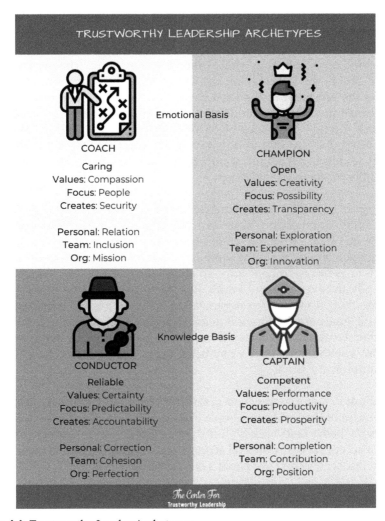

Figure 4.1 Trustworthy Leader Archetypes

them. These are two different approaches, but both have the same outcome: building trust with others.

THE FOUR ARCHETYPES OF TRUSTWORTHY LEADERS

The *Conductor* starts by demonstrating *Reliability*. They strongly value certainty, and consequently focus on achieving predictability in their interactions with others and the world in general. Their personal behavior creates accountability for themselves by showing up on time, getting the job done, and doing what they say they are going to do. By expecting others to do the same through their interpersonal behavior, they develop accountability in others as well.

Their goals are correction, team cohesion, and organizational perfection. Bob relayed how he performed this role at Parma:

> I ended up establishing what I called the "Key Four." That was me; Jay Dillon, the HR director; the chairman of the shop committee; and the president of the local union. Whenever we got into very difficult situations, I would call that group together and we would work through the issues or barriers to the change process. That gave me the opportunity to immediately communicate with these key leaders in the organization who had accountability and responsibility for these critical issues

The *Champion* begins by demonstrating *Openness*. They highly value creativity and flexibility, and therefore focus on possibilities rather than certainties when dealing with others. Their personal actions demonstrate greater transparency by being open about "what the score is" when others hesitate to do so. They often try to persuade others through storytelling or the use of vivid metaphors, and can be revealing to a fault. In expecting others to be similarly open, moreover, their team and/or organization achieves greater transparency as well. Their goals are exploration, team experimentation, and organizational innovation. Leaders have been shown to be trusted either by being transparent in the way that they lead[4] or by being open. Bob described how he acted as a Champion at Parma:

> I think it was my ability to grasp that the plant could save itself because of the skills our people had, and that the employees were simply being held back by our dysfunctional culture. Rather than just accepting that it was all screwed up, I realized that if we could get our act together, we could save this place.

The *Captain* conveys trustworthiness initially through *Competence*. They value excellence in performance a great deal, and because of this focus on productivity. Doing this themselves, and expecting the same of others, improves the bottom line for their team and organization. Their goals are completion, increasing their team's contribution, and enhancing their organization's competitive position. As Bob put it:

> I acted as a captain through my commitment to holding the quarterly business meeting with our thousands of employees. That was a very grueling, time-consuming requirement that I set up to accomplish every quarter. When I found out that the quarterly business meetings really weren't adequate, then I assigned Dave Nedrich to be the communication coordinator and we started the weekly Video Bob series, taking place between the quarterly business meetings. Video Bob was a nickname given to him because of so many communication videos. Bob loved it because it helped

bring a smile to everyone and a little levity to some very complex cultural changes.

These were used during team meetings across the plant to provide everyone with our most up-to-date information.

The *Coach* establishes trustworthiness initially through *Caring*. They strongly value compassion and, as a result, focus on understanding people and helping them with their needs, concerns, and interests while disdaining others' selfishness. They are therefore able to contribute to a sense of security for their followers, fostering a greater shared sense of purpose among their teammates, and contributing to the norm of reciprocity within their organization. Their goals are forming relations with others, creating stronger team inclusion, and fostering greater commitment to the organization's mission. Bob shared how he performed this role:

> My coaching was intended not to dehumanize or embarrass people but, quite the contrary, to restore their faith in themselves and look for opportunities to grow if they felt they lacked support or did not believe they had the capability to do something. Whatever hardship they had, I always took the approach that, whatever they had to say, I was there to listen, not to judge. Together, we would work out the best approach towards finding the solution.

Questions to Consider

- Which role do you currently play in your organization?
- Is there a role you would like to play, with more practice or intention?
- Which role do you look for in your mentor?

Notes

1. Jawahar, I. M., Stone, T. H., & Kluemper, D. (2019). When and why leaders trust followers: LMX as a mediator and empowerment as a moderator of the trustworthiness-trust relationship. *The Career Development International*, 24(7), 702–716.
2. McAllister, D. J. (1995). Affect- and cognition-based trust as foundations for interpersonal cooperation in organizations. *Academy of Management Journal*, 38(1), 24–59.
3. Here, we are using trust building and demonstrating trustworthiness interchangeably for the sake of brevity. In addition to demonstrating one's trustworthiness, there are obviously numerous ways to build trust, which we discuss in later chapters. The ROCC of Trust model is helpful for those other ways as well.
4. Norman, S. M., Avolio, B. J., & Luthans, F. (2010). The impact of positivity and transparency on trust in leaders and their perceived effectiveness. *The Leadership Quarterly*, 21(3), 350–364.

5 EACH LEADER NEEDS EMPATHY, AUTHENTICITY, COURAGE, AND HUMILITY

For Bob, it was the people that worked for him that kept him going into work every day. By the end of his first year, Bob and his hourly employees were making significant progress in a number of areas for which Bob was responsible. The biggest reason in Bob's mind was that he and his employees were working together as a team, whereas before Bob became their supervisor, they had not been involved in figuring out how to attain the goals set for them—indeed, it was quite the opposite.

Before Bob became their supervisor, the culture was such that most of these UAW-represented employees wanted to make life miserable for their supervisors and to do as little possible rather than giving their best efforts to the plant and to GM. Whenever any one of them would be disciplined for insubordination or other rule violations, the UAW would fight the charges, saying that they were being treated poorly by management. Nonetheless, management would almost always win, resulting in the employee being fired.

Despite the progress Bob was making with both his team and their results, the relentless criticism that he and his fellow supervisors received from bosses were taking their toll. Bob thought that if someone was being criticized for something they had done, or not done appropriately, then they would be given feedback on how to avoid repeating the error. Well, that very frequently did not happen. As Bob said, "It was more a case of, 'You *&%$up again,' or, 'Geez, how many #$@% times do I have to tell you?' Over time, I began to internalize their constant criticism." Bob had developed a great deal of empathy for his hourly employees because he was receiving the same unjustified treatment that they had received from their supervisors before Bob became their boss.

In terms of the ROCC of Trust, as important as leaders' trustworthiness is in order for others to trust them, leaders themselves also need to trust others if they want to foster change, often before they know whether their followers are trustworthy themselves. What makes it possible for them to do so are four key qualities, which we have labeled EACH: Empathy, Authenticity, Compassion, and Humility. As illustrated in Figure 5.1 (Mishra & Mishra, 2022), these qualities work together, and even balance each other by helping leaders know who they are. They also promote a leader's willingness and ability to build trust with others. None of the qualities by themselves is sufficient for effective leadership; indeed, by way of example, we can easily imagine an authentic jerk,

DOI: 10.4324/9780367822170-7

E.A.C.H. Model of Leadership

Figure 5.1 Four EACH Model of Leadership

or someone whose courage can become foolhardiness if not bounded by the other qualities.

Empathy, authenticity, courage, and humility have all been examined by scholars in the context of how they impact on a leader's ability to be effective in building trust with their employees. Empathy, for example, allows a leader to build trust with others by creating emotional bonds.[1] Authentic leaders have enough self-awareness to admit their limitations and show up in their role as a real person, a trait which followers admire and trust.[2] Courageous leaders act in the best interests of others, which in turn promotes ethical behavior in their followers.[3] Finally, humble leaders think less of themselves than others, which allows them to ask for help in solving problems or taking on a new challenge. This encourages others to be more open and, as a result, more trusting, due to the leader's willingness to work with them to achieve organizational goals.[4]

Having EACH makes it easier to create positive change by trusting others first before you have demonstrated your own trustworthiness in any significant way. In other words, you are "priming the pump" by trusting first and only subsequently becoming trusted. This will put you at risk for being vulnerable to the actions of others if they turn out not to be trustworthy. Those who are courageous enough to trust first find that this a way to become a trustworthy leader more readily.

In this chapter, we discuss how and why leaders are able to trust before being trusted. In subsequent chapters, we will return to this critical leadership capability and orientation. The genius of this is that by being smart about trusting others, rather than doing so without thinking, leaders are able to demonstrate the ROCC of Trust. Indeed, done intelligently, trusting is leadership oriented because by definition it involves interacting with others.

LEADING WITH EMPATHY

Empathy is defined as "our capacity to see the world through others' eyes, to feel what they feel ... experience what they experience."[5,6] This definition comprises the emotional and cognitive components of empathy as discussed by Stanford empathy researcher Jamil Zaki.[7] Empathic leaders will be more effective at engaging and retaining followers because they understand their needs, concerns, and aspirations. Such understanding includes both verbal and non-verbal messages.[8] Empathic leaders will also communicate in an interpersonally and informationally fair way.[9] Empathy does not have to lead to compassion, but compassion depends on empathy because understanding the situation another faces makes it easier to want to help if the situation calls for it. As Aneil's friend Larry Stimpert, president of Hampden-Sydney College, shared with us:

> At one of my institutions, one of our major academic buildings leaked every time it rained, affecting both faculty offices and classrooms. Faculty offices had mold, and large chunks of plaster were falling off the walls and ceilings. My boss walked past that building every day on his way to lunch, and so I said to him, 'You know, it would be great for the faculty morale if, once in a while, you'd simply walk through the building and tell people you understand the challenges, and 'we're going to get it fixed.'

But Larry's boss took this suggestion as a criticism of his leadership, or that he was trying to undermine is relationship with faculty members, rather than advising him to understand their concerns and act on them. As Larry put it succinctly, "*a big part of leadership is showing that you have empathy.*"

Empathic leaders are more likely to be trustworthy in terms of caring because understanding another's situation makes it easier to care about that person's needs and interests, and to want to help that other person if the situation calls for it. It is not a guarantee, however, nor should it be. Leaders need to be concerned with the welfare of their entire team or organization, and not be unduly influenced by any particular person's need for help if they are to be considered trustworthy by all of their followers. This applies not only in terms of caring, but of competence as well. A leader that goes too far in helping one person at the expense of the rest will undoubtedly undermine their ability to help the entire team or organization succeed. One of Aneil's former MBA students, Juan Carlos Sanchez, shared how he views the role of empathy:

> Empathy plays a key role in developing others as in order to build the foundation of a lasting and trusting relationship there's a need to communicate (and probably equally important to lead by example) clearly and frequently with those under my wing. It's also important to understand that because I'm helping develop other leaders, they don't necessarily have to have the same leadership

traits I have; however, there are certain elements that are common denominators among leaders (i.e., integrity, honesty, openness, etc.) that no matter what type of leaders they will turn out to be, these elements must always be there.

Building greater empathy is just one way of improving your EQ.[10] If you want to develop greater empathy, begin by imagining what it must be like to be in someone else's situation (choose a real-life situation). In addition, it always helps to reflect on how you handled a situation and perhaps ask for feedback if possible.[11] Dr. Anitra Manning of IBM shared how she has focused on positive self-development through journaling:

> I began the process of daily self-reflection early in my career. Back then, I was commuting for about two hours roundtrip daily on the Long Island Railroad. During my ride home, I closed out my final emails, powered down my smart phone, and pulled out my journal. I began a fresh page by answering my self-authored daily prompts: "What was that day like for you? What were the things that brought you joy, stress? What could you do better the next day?"

> It was a way for me to analyze my productivity and my efficacy as a leader. By the time that I arrived to my home station, I finished my analysis, released the day, and was prepared for the next day. I could descend the station stairwell with a smile as I looked forward to my evening with my family. That was a practice that I did early-on that I think was very helpful. I did the same thing over the years. When I stopped doing that, I felt the stress come back. Stress and burnout are real phenomena; best managed by asking for support and self-compassion/nurturing practices. These ways of being are essential and must not be compromised.

As a result of Bob's early experience leading hourly employees, he decided that when he became a plant manager he would eliminate as many artificial distinctions between hourly and salaried employees as possible, including different dress codes, especially wearing ties—something Bob thought symbolized all that was wrong with GM's inflexible hierarchy. He would also remove more substantive distinctions, such as separate parking lots and cafeterias for hourly and salaried employees and salaried managers.

LEADING WITH AUTHENTICITY

An authentic leader is one who lives the values that they espouse. Authentic leaders have greater self-awareness, are guided by a strong set of morals, relate transparently with others, and focus on positive self-development.[12,13] Authentic leaders are not perceived as being hypocritical, because no gaps or differences are discernible between their words and their actions.[14] They are also "perceived by others as being aware of their own and others' values or moral perspectives."[15] Of course, we are assuming that the leader's values or morality are in keeping with those of both their followers and the society in which they live, and that they are not harmful. Clearly, a leader who is greedy, dishonest, or favors certain employees is unlikely to win over many followers, no matter how authentically these negative values are displayed.

Authenticity enhances trust building in many ways. It opens up the leader to being influenced by others and to meeting their needs.[16] Authentic leaders also have high physical and mental energy and persevere in the face of obstacles and difficulties.[17] They view personal failures and setbacks as temporary, onetime occurrences, as well as learning experiences.[18] They are therefore more likely to want to trust others even if their trust is violated by some people. Authentic leaders are highly self-motivated and more likely to set stretch goals for themselves and others.[19]

Empathy and authenticity balance each other. If a leader is too empathetic, they run the danger of overly identifying with their subordinates or followers, and not balancing their needs with those of the team or organization. Authenticity without empathy can easily lead to narcissism. You can learn more about the role of trust, authenticity, humility, and courage in a chapter we have written which provides further detail.[20]

LEADING WITH COURAGE

Leading with courage is about your willingness to confront the status quo,[21] your confidence about the future,[22] and confidence about your ability to make a difference. Our friend Dr. Gerry McNamara of MSU and his colleagues found in their research that self-reflection can improve one's leadership by visualizing and reflecting on "your best leader self," thereby instilling greater self-confidence and the courage to act.[23] Followers need to have hope for the future if they are going to contribute to organizational change efforts, and leaders who have courage are more capable of conveying that hope to others. It is hope, rather than optimism, that is more closely related to trust and more likely to engender action, especially when circumstances are uncertain or even threatening. Optimism reflects a general, positive expectation about the future, irrespective of one's own actions. Hope, on the other hand, is an emotion that reflects the belief that one is capable of securing a successful and fulfilling future.[24,25] Innovative leaders score higher on managing risk, demonstrating curiosity, confidence, and seizing opportunities.[26] Courageous leaders, then, are more likely to engender hope because through their own belief in their abilities to make a difference; they can encourage their followers to develop similar beliefs.

Leaders who possess greater courage are more likely to build trust with others.[27] One reason for this is that leaders who are more self-confident are more trusting in general,[28] which in turn makes them more likely to build trust with others. For example, we know it takes courage to admit we made a mistake. Leaders with greater courage will be more likely to admit to and rectify their mistakes, thereby building trust with others. Leaders who are willing to confront the status quo are more likely to elicit cooperation from others, and this cooperation is enhanced by the trust the leader has built. When the leader has confidence in the future, they will want to develop the trust necessary to convince others to co-create such a future together. Our colleague Jenny Meyer shared how she embraces courage in the workplace:

> Courage, for me personally, means sometimes getting up every day. It means speaking up. I'm surrounded by engineers and operators who are far more experienced in the industry than I am. I must practice courage to tell my team members, 'that's not a good idea.'

LEADING WITH HUMILITY

Leading with humility is defined as "a desirable personal quality reflecting the willingness to understand the self (identities, strengths, limitations), combined with perspective in the self's relationships with others (i.e., the perspective that one is not the center of the universe)."[29] Leaders who are humble are aware of their limitations and openly discuss them with others. After all, self-aware leaders must understand how others perceive them.[30] This openness helps the leader to ensure they are moving in the right direction.[31] Humble leaders are also aware of how others perceive them and try to integrate these perceptions with their own self-perceptions.[32] Humble leaders can foster a sense of shared fate by acknowledging that they do not have all the answers and need help from their followers, especially in times of crisis.

Humble leaders are also more likely to build trust with others because they are open to feedback—which itself is a potentially vulnerable and trusting act. Humility motivates leaders to seek followers because they recognize they cannot do it alone. It also bounds courage so that it does not become arrogance. Clearly, humility can be developed in leaders,[33] and our work shows that early developmental experiences and failures or mistakes are the important developers of humility—we discuss some examples in Chapter 6.

One way in which leaders demonstrate both reliability and competence through trusting is by delegating to others. It is much easier to fulfill commitments and accomplish objectives if a leader has help from others. By sharing critical information, the leader is not only trusting the recipients of that information, but also demonstrating openness. Finally, by helping others who are in need, leaders are trusting them—considering they could be taken advantage of—but in doing so they are also demonstrating caring. By trusting others first, leaders also skillfully model to their followers how to trust, so that the culture of trust we discuss later in Part III of this book begins to develop straightaway.

As you move through your career from investing in yourself to developing teams and to building a culture of trust, we elaborate how this can be accomplished effectively through intentional leadership and the EACH foundation.

Questions to Consider

- Which of the EACH characteristics come naturally to you? Why is that?
- Which of the EACH characteristics is less comfortable for you? What can you do to develop those characteristics as an intentional leader?
- Do you have any role models in your life for EACH characteristic? How can their example help you develop them in yourself?

Notes

1. Tzouramani, E. (2017). Leadership and empathy. Springer Texts in Business and Economics, In: J. Marques, & S. Dhiman (Eds.), *Leadership today* (pp. 197–216), Springer.
2. Henderson, J. E. (2015). Leader authenticity: A renewed call for research. *Journal of Leadership, Accountability & Ethics, 12*(2).
3. Hannah, S. T., Avolio, B. J., & Walumbwa, F. O. (2011). Relationships between authentic leadership, moral courage, and ethical and pro-social behaviors. *Business Ethics Quarterly, 21*(4), 555–578.
4. Schein, E. H., & Schein, P. A. (2018). *Humble leadership: The power of relationships, openness, and trust.* Berrett-Koehler Publishers.
5. Bloom, P. (2016). *Against empathy: The case for rational compassion.* HarperCollins. Kindle edition, locations 164, 187.
6. Patient, D. L., & Skarlicki, D. P. (2010). Increasing interpersonal and informational justice when communicating negative news: The role of the manager's empathic concern and moral development. *Journal of Management, 36*(2), 555–578.
7. Zaki, J. (2019). *The war for kindness: Building empathy in fractured world.* Crown Publishing Group.
8. Polychroniou, P. V. (2009). Relationship between emotional intelligence and transformational leadership of supervisors: The impact on team effectiveness. *Team Performance Management: An International Journal,* 343–356.
9. Patient, D. L., & Skarlicki, D. P. (2010). Increasing interpersonal and informational justice when communicating negative news: The role of the manager's empathic concern and moral development. *Journal of Management, 36*(2), 555–578.
10. Goleman, D. (2005). *Emotional intelligence.* Bantam.
11. Bariso, J. (2018). *EQ applied: The real-world guide to emotional intelligence: How to make emotions work for you, instead of against you.* Borough Hall.
12. Nielsen, R., Marrone, J. A., & Slay, H. S. (2010). A new look at humility: Exploring the humility concept and its role in socialized charismatic leadership (SCL). *Journal of Leadership & Organizational Studies, 17*(1), 33–43.
13. Owens, B. P., Rowatt, W. C., & Wilkins, A. L. (2012). Exploring the relevance and implications of humility in organizations. In K. S. Cameron, & G. M. Spreitzer (Eds.), *Handbook of positive organizational scholarship* (pp. 260–272). Oxford University Press.
14. Walumbwa, F. O., Avolio, B. J., Gardner, W. L., Wernsing, T. S., & Peterson, S. J. (2008). Authentic leadership: Development and validation of a theory-based measure. *Journal of Management, 34*(1), 89–126.

15. Luthans, F., & Avolio, B. (2003). Authentic leadership development. In K. S. Cameron, S. E. Dutton, & R. E. Quinn (Eds.), *Positive organizational scholarship—Foundations of a new discipline* (pp. 241–258). Berrett-Koehler Publishers.

16. Mishra, A. & Mishra, K. (2012). Trust in leaders and lasting positive change. In K. S. Cameron, & G. M. Spreitzer (Eds.), *Handbook of positive organizational scholarship* (pp. 449–461). Oxford University Press.

17. Luthans, F., & Avolio, B. (2003). Authentic leadership development. In K. S. Cameron, S. E. Dutton, & R. E. Quinn (Eds.), *Positive organizational scholarship—Foundations of a new discipline* (pp. 241–258). Berrett-Koehler Publishers.

18. Luthans, F., & Avolio, B. (2003). Authentic leadership development. In K. S. Cameron, S. E. Dutton, & R. E. Quinn (Eds.), *Positive organizational scholarship—Foundations of a new discipline* (pp. 241–258). Berrett-Koehler Publishers.

19. Luthans, F., & Avolio, B. (2003). Authentic leadership development. In K. S. Cameron, S. E. Dutton, & R. E. Quinn (Eds.), *Positive organizational scholarship—Foundations of a new discipline* (pp. 241–258). Berrett-Koehler Publishers.

20. Mishra, A. K., & Mishra, K. E. (2012). Trust and positive organizational leadership. In K. S. Cameron, & G. M. Spreitzer (Eds.), *The Oxford handbook of positive organizational scholarship*. Oxford University Press.

21. Mishra, A. K., & Mishra, K. E. (2008). *Trust is everything: Become the leader others will follow*. Lulu.

22. Norman, S. M., Avolio, B. J., & Luthans, F. (2010). The impact of positivity and transparency on trust in leaders and their perceived effectiveness. *The Leadership Quarterly, 21*(3), 350–364.

23. Jennings, R. E., Klodiana, L., Lanaj, Koopman, J., & McNamara, G. (2021). Reflecting on one's best possible self as a leader: Implications for professional employees at work, *Personnel Psychology,* 1–22. https://onlinelibrary.wiley.com/doi/epdf/10.1111/peps.12447?saml_referrer

24. Alarcon, G. M., Bowling, N. A., & Khazon, S. (2013). Great expectations: A meta-analytic examination of optimism and hope. *Personality and Individual Differences, 54*(7/May), 821–827.

25. Dholakia, U. (2017, February 26). *What's the difference between optimism and hope?* Psychology Today. https://www.psychologytoday.com/us/blog/the-science-behind-behavior/201702/whats-the-difference-between-optimism-and-hope

26. Graham-Leviss, K. (2016, December 20). *The 5 skills that innovative leaders have in common.* Harvard Business Review. https://hbr.org/2016/12/the-5-skills-that-innovative-leaders-have-in-common

27. Worline, M. C., & Quinn, R. (2003). Positive organizational scholarship: Foundations of a new discipline. In K. Cameron, J. Dutton, & R. Quinn (Eds.), *Positive organizational scholarship: Foundations of a new discipline* (pp. 138–161). Berrett-Koehler Publishers.

28. Luthans, F., & Avolio, B. (2003). Authentic leadership development. In K. Cameron, J. Dutton, & R. Quinn (Eds.) *Positive organizational scholarship: Foundations of a new discipline* (pp. 240–258). Berrett-Koehler Publishers.

29. Mishra, A., & Mishra, K. (2008). *Trust is everything: Become the leader others will follow.* Lulu.

30. Chon, D., and Sitkin, S. B. (2021). Disentangling the process and content of self-awareness: A review, critical assessment, and synthesis. *Academy of Management Annals, 15*(2), 607–651.

31. Rotter, J. B. (1967). A new scale for the measurement of interpersonal trust. *Journal of Personality, 35*(4), 651–65.

32. Nielsen, R., Marrone, J. A., & Slay, H. S. (2010). A new look at humility: Exploring the humility concept and its role in socialized charismatic leadership (SCL). *Journal of Leadership & Organizational Studies, 17*(1), 33–43.

33. Luthans, F., & Avolio, B. (2003). Authentic leadership development. In K. S. Cameron, S. E. Dutton, & R. E. Quinn (Eds.), *Positive organizational scholarship— Foundations of a new discipline* (pp. 241–258). Berrett-Koehler Publishers.

6

LEADING **FROM** YOUR STRENGTHS

At the beginning of Bob's career, he said his success was dependent on 80% technical skills and 20% people skills; by the time he became plant manager, it had become 20% technical and 80% people skills. As a first-line supervisor, he had enough technical know-how to help his employees get their machines working again—for example, to get a conveyor restarted. But as he moved up the management ranks, he could not possibly keep up with all the technological changes in the operations he used to supervise, much less all the new operations which had come under his responsibility. Equally important, he really enjoyed the "people side of the business": supporting those who worked for him; those whose work ethic he admired; and those he could help do an even better job through training or by providing any additional resources they needed, accelerating their productivity and improving quality as a result.

Still, the work was exhausting. He was working 10- to 12-hour days, mentally worn out because the situations that he had to work through almost always started out highly negatively charged, often with years of conflict that had preceded his arrival as the new plant manager. Some of that conflict was due to the way his predecessors had treated the employees he now led. Some of it was simply because the problems were complex and the people working on them had "different attitudes, different backgrounds," and came from "different schools of thought."

Bob told us that getting these very different people to agree upon the best approach, and to arrive at solutions where everybody wins, was always his goal. This was not easy, though, especially when they had been arguing with each other for a long time before Bob showed up. Bob says, "No matter what size group it was, I wanted everybody to feel comfortable in the direction that we were taking." Early on, he had not had any training in conflict management or leading teams, so it was his personal approach coupled with the few leadership skills he had developed up to that point:

> I had to work through each situation in the best way I could until we had people smiling again, looking to move ahead in a positive rather than argumentative manner. That occurred every day. It took a lot of energy, but I had a deep sense of pride, confidence in my ability to change the culture, and was dedicated to it, even though it came at the expense of time with my family. There were a lot of times I would come home and the kids were already in bed. But

DOI: 10.4324/9780367822170-8

I wanted our plant to succeed. I wanted to make it the best plant within GM, and let GM know that it could be done.

Leadership can be lonely, which is why you have to start by investing in yourself. Using your strengths is a positive way to build trust. Similarly, acknowledging your weaknesses is another way in which to build trust. When we acknowledge that we do not know the answer to everything, our colleagues will trust us more than if we convey that we "know it all." As Mike Gannon put it:

> I am sure I started with some inherent leadership abilities, but mostly I developed my leadership style through making lots of mistakes. While I never wrote anything down, I did have a sort of mental "checklist" of hard-learned lessons that I referred to.

One way we have found to be very effective for investing in yourself is to take Gallup's Clifton Strengths Assessment.[1] The Clifton Strengths Assessment is inexpensive, quick to take, and provides you with your top five strengths, or ways that you prefer to work and lead. When you get the results and identify your strengths, you will better understand why you have been successful and happy in your work, or why you may be struggling and dissatisfied. Using your strengths is a great way to demonstrate trustworthiness, because they are an authentic, genuine way to contribute excellence as an individual as well as with your team and organization. Knowing how to use your top five strengths can help you be a better leader immediately.

When we coach young leaders, we find that they are not surprised as they first read about their strengths. Often, young leaders take their strengths for granted and think that everyone has these same qualities. A better way to look at your strengths is to realize that you already have five powerful ways to lead yourself and others that your peers may not have.

The assessment results also provide the basis for getting coached and for coaching others. The best employees are coachable, and the Clifton Strengths Assessment makes coaching a positive experience. We will focus more on coaching in Part II, but in the meantime, know that even professionals at the top of their game seek out coaching in order to take their performance, even leadership performance, to a higher level.

In a highly cited article in *The New Yorker*, Atul Gawande, MD, prescribes coaching as a good way to improve any professional career. He describes good coaches as those who listen more than they talk. In addition, they have an ability to "make a personal connection and focus little on themselves." As he, himself worked with a coach, he felt that his coach was "one hundred per cent present in the conversation." Finally, his coach was able to parcel out his observations carefully. "It's not a normal way of communicating—watching what your words are doing," he said.[2] As Dr. Bruce Rubin stated, "recognize that becoming a good leader takes time and effort and remaining a good leader is a continuous investment."[3]

BE A POSITIVE LEADER

One other way to make an investment in yourself is to strive to be a positive leader. In his book *Positive Leadership* our mentor from the Ross School of Business at the University of Michigan Dr. Kim Cameron describes a positive leader as "one who 1) aims to help individuals and organizations attain spectacular levels of achievement; 2) focuses on strategies that provide strengths-based, positive energy to individuals and organizations; and 3) fosters virtuousness."[4]

According to Dr. Cameron, individuals develop themselves into positive leaders by modeling and encouraging acts of compassion, forgiveness, and gratitude.[5] You do not need a formal title to do this. In his research on positive organizations and leaders, Dr. Cameron has found that leaders who provide more supportive, encouraging and appreciative comments to team members (as opposed to negative comments) end up with more positive outcomes. Again, these acts are not something you need a formal title for before you can put them into action.

SEEK OUT MENTORS

Finding a mentor can be a positive way to build your confidence and get a new perspective on your career. Some organizations have formal mentoring programs in place to connect new employees with mentors. If yours does not, you might seek out an informal mentor either from within your organization or even outside of it.

As Dr. Anitra Manning of IBM told us, a mentor can introduce you to other mentors, helping you to build your network.

> I have benefited from formal and informal mentors. I have had informal mentors introduce me to those who would become lifetime mentors. I have had mentors that have given me timely and honest feedback, helped me problem-solve, guided my career, prepared me for interviews, and have introduced me to sponsors. My first formal mentor was my high school principal, Dr. Barbara Thompson, with a stream of mentors within and outside of the workplace. Mentors and coaches are essential in the life of a leader.

When you find a positive mentoring relationship, it can improve your attitude towards your work and your career.[6] Steve Fitzgerald described just how critical one of his mentors was to him:

> I'll never forget her, and I'll thank her till the last day that I breathe. There was a union rep at the Sheldon Road plant when I was a labor rep. It was four months after I had arrived as a very junior, wet-behind-the-ears person. My job at Ford was sort of the trial-by-fire-thing, as it is for all young HR people. You're thrust in there,

you're given a whole pile of grievances to adjudicate, and every day you're dealing with elected UAW reps who had been in their roles for 15 years before you got there and will be there for a decade after you leave.

I was just a mess. I was trying to win every battle. I was pulling out the contract all the time, something that these people had seen time and again. One day Marie closed my door after we had a tumultuous session, and she said, "Okay, kid, enough. Meet me at Miller's for lunch, and we're going to talk." Miller's was a Dearborn icon where they served their burgers on wax paper. A who's who of Ford Motor Company would come through there every day. We sat there for four hours, went through a bunch of beer, and she gave me a lesson in practical politics.

Kid, you've got all the advantages that none of us have. You're going to be doing things that none of us will have a chance to do. We've been here forever. You're going to forget all about us. We're still going to be here building machines. I got out of that [trap] by becoming a union rep, and my future is dependent upon getting reelected.

By supporting her when she needed it, I helped her improve the competitiveness of this plant because she understood that the union needed to change or else everyone was going to be out of work. She just gave me a lesson in how there was a whole level of conversation going on that I was blind to. From that day forward, I was a much better human, and I was a hell of a lot of a better executive down the road because I had learned that very early in my life.

JOIN A NONPROFIT BOARD

Another way you can develop yourself while helping others is to join a nonprofit board. Many nonprofit organizations welcome people with business backgrounds to help them review budgets, improve marketing, and increase their fundraising and/or volunteer base. If there are areas at work that you want to move into (for instance, you work in accounting now, but want to move into marketing), serving on a nonprofit board is a great way to get the experience you need to help you prepare for a different role at your company. It also gives you the pride and satisfaction of helping a local organization that needs your expertise.

Questions to Consider

- In what ways do you invest in yourself today?
- How can you find a mentor if your organization does not have a formal mentoring program?
- Whom can you mentor?

Notes

1. https://www.gallup.com/cliftonstrengths/en/home.aspx
2. Gawande, A. (2011, October 3). *Personal best: Top athletes and singers have coaches. Should you?* The New Yorker. https://www.newyorker.com/magazine/2011/10/03/personal-best
3. Mishra, A. K. & Mishra, K. E. (2013). *Becoming a trustworthy leader: Psychology and practice.* Routledge, 31.
4. Cameron, K. (2012). *Positive leadership: Strategies for extraordinary performance* (p. 2–3). Berrett-Koehler Publishers.
5. Cameron, K. (2012). *Positive leadership: Strategies for extraordinary performance* (p. 22). Berrett-Koehler Publishers.
6. Ragins, B. R., Cotton, J. L., & Miller, J. S. (2000). Marginal mentoring: The effects of type of mentor, quality of relationship, and program design on work and career attitudes. *Academy of Management Journal, 43*(6), 1177–1194.

7 REIMAGINE YOURSELF AND YOUR CAREER

One evening, after Bob had been at GM for a little over a year, his wife, Karen, asked him once again how his day had gone. Bob told her once again how frustrating it was to work for GM. She replied, "Every day you come home and I ask you the question, hoping you're going to say, 'I had a wonderful day,' but you don't. If you're this unhappy, it's a big world, you're young, you've got a good education. You can go wherever you want to go." Bob replied, "Well, that sounds easy." Karen advised, "Well, my suggestion is either you commit to a more positive approach to what you're doing or just quit and we'll go someplace else." After recounting this story, Bob told us, "There are a lot of things I don't remember in my career, but I remember that night because I knew she was right. It was excellent advice."

Bob had already seen other supervisors leave, which in his mind took some gumption. He wondered what held him back from taking advantage of his youth and the opportunities that were available to college graduates. It was the early 1960s, and Bob knew that "excellent jobs at major corporations were very, very plentiful."

But during the middle of that night, he decided that there was enough that he liked about his work that he was going to take a more positive attitude, to not let things bother him as much. He reminisced, "Because I never responded to the poor ways in which management treated me, I internalized their relentlessly negativism. It bothered me that I had done this, so from then on I decided to insulate myself from their unjustified judgments."

To reimagine yourself takes a healthy dose of courage. It also takes the ability to appreciate your authentic self and know how you can use your strengths to improve your job and excel in your career. As Professor Herminia Ibarra describes in her book *Working Identity*, we do not suddenly wake up one day and make a change without considering the alternatives. She describes the process of reinvention as having several parts:

1. We start by updating our priorities.
2. We then move on to explore our possible selves.
3. We linger between both identities.
4. We finally make an actual career change, while also internally changing our focus and finding congruence between who we are and what we do.[1]

A leader we have long admired, Ted Castle, owner and President of Rhino Foods, was working the counter at Chessy's Frozen Custard, the small

DOI: 10.4324/9780367822170-9

Burlington, Vermont ice cream and deli store that he and his wife, Anne, had started a 40 years earlier. As he handed out another ice cream cone to a customer, the person recognized him and said, *"aren't you Ted Castle?"* Ted's face brightened until the customer then said, *"weren't you supposed to get the head coaching job at UVM?"*

Yes, indeed. It was 1986, and Ted had been an All-American and captain of the University of Vermont's (UVM) ice hockey team during the previous decade. He had graduated in 1974, after winning back-to-back ECAC Division II titles.[2] He then played professional ice hockey for two years in Sweden and Italy before taking assistant coaching jobs, first at the University of Maine and then at UVM. He then was passed over for the head coaching job. Ted recalls, "At least I could go work with my wife when I didn't get the UVM coaching job. Luckily, we had started doing a wholesale business, so I could focus on making cookie dough for our wholesale customers and not keep being asked why I hadn't gotten the head coaching job."

While the business was still small but growing, Ted had to make use of equipment owned by his friends:

> I would take my cart with all my cookie dough ingredients— eggs, flour, and sugar—up the elevator to use a mixer in a restaurant owned by my friend. After that, I would then take the cookie dough mix across the street to a grocery store to use its ovens to make my cookies. Then I'd come back and make my little ice cream cookie sandwiches, wrap them up and put them in my car, and drive across town and put them into customers' freezers. That was about the extent of our business plan.

On one of these days, while he was transporting his cookie dough ingredients to mix them, the elevator door opened and as he pushed the cart out, his tray of 30 eggs fell and broke. The eggs started to drip through the crack between the elevator and the floor. Three ladies waiting to get on the elevator door gave Ted a questioning look, as if to say, "Do you know what you're doing?"[3] In recalling this incident, Ted said, "I think things happen in your life for a reason. That's when I decided I had to grow my wholesale business so that I could afford my own equipment and wouldn't have to keep spilling eggs everywhere in front of people."

Even as Rhino Foods continued to grow, Ted realized that he really wasn't into it in the same way as when he'd coached. "Business was going all right, but I really didn't have a passion for it. I figured that I needed to find a way to go at this hard, like I do most things, or I should just get out of it. That is when I decided to think of the company as a team and set higher expectations for the company, myself and the employees."

Ted's early lack of passion for running his company provided a way to empathize with his employees, who were similarly uninspired because they only thought of their jobs as making money for Ted and Anne. They did not see any connection between giving the company their best effort and building a future for themselves that they could be proud of. In demonstrating courage by reinventing his career, Ted would similarly challenge his employees to think and act as though they were owners instead of the employees. He motivated them to think and act this way by developing a performance management and reward system that would get them to think and act as owners. We will see later on that he developed this in a way that was authentic and consistent with his experience of playing and coaching hockey. It would make working at Rhino be like playing a rewarding game in which everyone could win. Ted was also humble enough to recognize that his employees were the key to the company's success, and that he needed their help to innovate and grow.

The next part will focus on leading teams, which is very different than leading oneself, but which also critically depends on being able to build and use the ROCC of Trust.

Questions to Consider

- When have you turned disappointment into something positive?
- How can you see the long-term perspective as Bob did and then act for the good of your team or organization?
- How can you now reimagine your job/career/skillset as Ted did in order to make a difference for yourself and your team?

Notes

1. Ibarra, H. (2004). *Working identity: Unconventional strategies for reinventing your career.* Harvard Business Press.
2. The ECAC was an intercollege ice hockey league. Division II of the league comprised those colleges which offered athletic scholarships.
3. From Mishra, A.K. & Mishra, K. E. *Trust is everything: Become the leader others will follow.* 2008. Lulu. Used with permission.

LEADING TEAMS (EMPOWERING OTHERS TO BE TRUSTWORTHY)

8 THE IMPORTANCE OF TEAMWORK

Part II focuses on how to be an intentional *team* leader. We first discuss the attributes of a great team and why teams still need great leadership in order to accomplish their goals. We review how knowing each other's strengths can help team members work well together. Based on our own work with teams, we had a discussion how a coaching leadership style that appreciates team members' strengths and allows them to use them in their job on a regular basis is more effective than a directive style. With more teams working remotely, we share advice from other leaders on how to engage and empower teams in a remote work setting.

As Bob sought to change the culture of his very first team, he decided to begin working on engaging an employee who was critical to the effectiveness of Bob's operations but who was completely disengaged.

Bob had been on his first job for perhaps two or three weeks when a section of machinery broke down. He had learned of a skilled, bright machine repairman on his team who could fix it quickly, but could not find him. Looking around, Bob found a little cubby hole in the vast plant "about the size of an outhouse but outfitted more like a penthouse." It had a tiny table, bookshelves, and a lamp. The repairman was in there reading and drinking coffee, something Bob had not yet been able to sneak in that morning. Bob had no idea that he had been hiding out there.

Bob thought this person's job would be to keep things running and doing preventive maintenance, but the machine repairman did not see it that way. He saw his job as "when it's broke, I'll go fix it. In the meantime, I'm just going to sit here and do what I want to do." That was the way he operated. It took Bob a while to convince him that that was not what he was getting paid for, or what Bob expected of him. He simply asked, "Can't we work out a schedule where you're doing daily equipment maintenance so that it doesn't break down?" It took some time, but the repairman eventually came around to that way of thinking and became a valuable member of Bob's team.

Another member of Bob's team was a metal finisher by the name of John Gibson. He was 65 years old and ready to retire. John knew who had a good work ethic and who did not on Bob's team. He treated Bob like a grandson, giving him tips on how to handle each person. Bob recalls:

> It was those individuals and others like them who had a very significant impact on my approach to leadership. Unlike the employees

DOI: 10.4324/9780367822170-11

on my team, many of my managers saw me and my fellow new college grads as a threat to their promotions rather than an advantage for GM. Their attitude was, "You didn't pay your dues and gone through hell like we did." It was extremely difficult working for them, but I was still feeling good many days because of the accomplishments my team was making.

We spend most of our lives in teams of one type or another, whether it is our family, an athletic team while growing up, teams during our careers, or volunteer teams outside of work. Despite such ubiquity, people may belong to work teams without having any formal preparation or training. In order to understand how teams are defined, we have adopted Katzenbach and Smith's (1992) definition: A team is "a small number of people with complementary skills who are committed to a common purpose, set of performance goals, and approach for which they hold themselves mutually accountable."[1] Work teams are composed of interdependent individuals who share responsibility for specific outcomes in their organizations. Such teams are influenced by the context in which they are working,[2,3] all while producing "something useful to an organization."[4,5]

Teams are also the most typical way people in organizations come together to produce organizational outcomes. Thirty-one percent of employees say that most or all work is done in teams.[6] There are work teams, project teams, virtual teams, and formal and informal teams. The importance of teamwork matters as much in small firms as it does in large ones, like GM. Brooke Wilson, co-owner of several franchises of Two Men and a Truck, shared how she and her husband, Les, have built a trusted team together:

> A "chess player" who analyzes potential outcomes of every move and attempts to control direction may be a great asset to the team. But, without a "baseball player" who understands you can't wait for the ball to cross the plate before you swing, the team may be too slow to execute, and opportunities may be missed. This is how Les and I balance each other.

Implemented properly, teams can have a significant positive financial impact on an organization's bottom line.[7] Fifty-three percent of employees say that shifting to a team-based approach to work improves performance, but most rewards within organizations are still individually based.[8] Hundreds of studies have documented what contributes to team performance. How the team thinks about itself matters, because as with individuals, team self-efficacy enhances team performance.[9] Teams are an effective way to get work done in organizations.[10] Collectively, a team brings more creativity, knowledge, and experience to solving challenging problems than any one individual alone.[11] Moreover, as Figure 8.1 illustrates (Mishra & Mishra, 2022) the teams that share leadership, respect each other's area of expertise, and are able to build

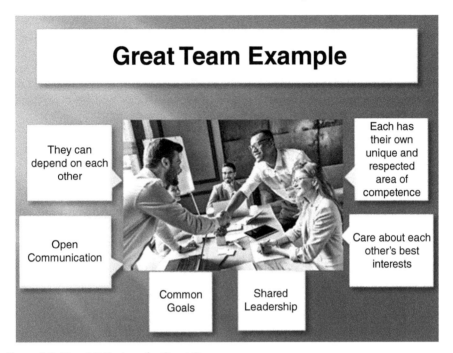

Great Team Example

They can depend on each other

Each has their own unique and respected area of competence

Open Communication

Care about each other's best interests

Common Goals

Shared Leadership

Figure 8.1 Key Attributes of a Great Team

the ROCC of Trust—show that they are reliable, open and honest, competent, and caring—are able to perform well.[12]

Once you have invested in yourself to become a leader and a strong team contributor, you will feel prepared to lead a team. Leaders can influence many aspects of team outcomes, including coordination, creativity, team learning, empowerment, commitment, team satisfaction, and performance.[13] Team members rely on their leader for structure, appreciation, and support. Cybersecurity expert Phil Wilhelm described how he creates a new team:

> When I am putting a new team together, I look for people who are comfortable in their own skin. I want them to be an authentic part of the team. Then, I ask myself if we are able to build authentic relationships and have "courageous conversations" with each other. If this is the case, then these are the people who will be on my team.

The leader of a team is not necessarily the same person for the lifespan of the team. On one end of the continuum is a team with a formally appointed leader. At the other end is a purely self-managed team (SMT) with no formal leader, with the leadership shifting depending on the team's tasks and goals. Team leaders can either be appointed from outside or from within the team, the latter being more expected for a SMT.[14] Indeed, a team with a formally appointed leader may evolve into a SMT as the team becomes more experienced and achieves a significant level of expertise.[15] Indeed, shared leadership has been found to enhance team performance,[16] and our own recent research demonstrates that the benefits of such shared leadership even extend to top management teams.[17] However, for this book, our focus will be individuals who are formally charged with leading a team.

As our GM mentor Mike Gannon put it:

> In my mid-teens, I had a conversation with my father about the Navy's practice of holding a ship's captain responsible for everything that happened aboard the ship. I had just read an article about a ship running aground and the how the captain had been held responsible. It seemed very unfair to me, and my dad—a retired Navy Reserve captain—seemed the perfect person to ask about it.
>
> He explained that the captain's job was to make sure that the ship was safe. If the navigator made a mistake, the captain should have made sure he was properly trained, or that someone checked his work. If the weather was bad, then the proper precautions were taken. But most of all, the captain should be on the bridge if the ship faced even the slightest chance of peril.
>
> The concept of being responsible for everything on my "watch" really resonated with me, even at that young age. Then as now, if someone on my team makes a mistake or has a poor result, I feel responsible for allowing it to happen. I know that there is always something I could have done to prevent it, be it better training, better direction, or better follow-up. When the "ship" is in peril, I need to always be on the bridge to support my crew.

Mike also built trust in his team by sharing credit. Whenever anyone on the team did a good job, Mike was quick to publicly praise them, whether to fellow personnel staffers or top division executives. Mike was secure enough in his own abilities and success that he did not need to claim credit for his subordinates' achievements. Smart people would know, in any case, that the effectiveness of those who reported to Mike was due in part to the mentoring and coaching he provided to his employees.

TRUST IS ESSENTIAL TO EFFECTIVE TEAMWORK

"Effective communications, goal attainment, and service attainment are possible only in an atmosphere of trust."[18] High mutual trust within teams enhances team performance by increasing members' engagement and focus on team tasks,[19] and compels members to assist one another when needed.[20] Trust is also important to developing shared goals, exchanging information fully, and sharing power among team members, all of which contribute to a team's performance.[21,22,23] TASCO vice president Jim McCown described how he built a trusted team:

> My team trusted me because they were able to experience over time that I would do what I say, and I expected them to do the same. They saw me give them credit for our wins and speak highly of their efforts, commitment, and results. They sensed that I put them first and that their success mattered to me.

One key approach for building trust within teams is for team members to learn how to listen actively to one another. Authors Gibson and Cohen noted that "active listening is particularly helpful in teams when some members come from high-context organizations (strong cultures) and others come from low-context organizations (weak cultures)" because this listening technique allows greater clarification[24] and knowledge sharing.[25] Listening is the most used but least taught communication skill we use at work.

When we ask our MBA students if they have ever taken a listening course, most say they never had any training. This is probably why it is the one of the most commonly requested courses we teach in our executive programs. To listen to a colleague or team member takes time and patience, which is why not everyone enjoys it. Employees tell us that this is one thing that they appreciate most in a leader: someone who will stop everything, give their full attention when they need to share important information, and listen to them.

Trust is essential for team behavior and continuing successful work,[26,27] but too much trust may make it difficult for the team to monitor itself to ensure optimal performance.[28,29] This is why the team leader is so important. The leader needs to be vigilant in holding team members accountable to one another and to the team's goals.

Developing trust within a team critically depends on the team's leader,[30] since a team leader's trust in other team members positively influences group members' trust in one another.[31] This is because team members look to the leader for an indication that other team members can be trusted, and then they act accordingly. Team leaders can also influence team performance through team trust.[32] Our GM mentor Mike Gannon recalled how influential his Boy Scout experience was in learning how to lead teams:

> My brother Tom likes to say that everything he learned about being a leader he learned as a senior patrol leader in the Boy Scouts. I totally agree with him.
>
> Between the ages of 11 and 17 I was in the Boy Scouts. We had a troop of about 25 boys, and Seymour—as he wanted us to call him—was our main adult leader. In addition to the adult leaders, one of the scouts was elected the youth leader and had the title of senior patrol leader. As a senior patrol leader, you had absolutely no power, but you were expected to get the other boys—including those that might be older than you—to follow your direction and accomplish important things.

After a few years, I was elected senior patrol leader. On the first camping trip in my new role, I used the default leadership style of all young men: yelling! Needless to say, I was a complete failure.

Seymour took me aside and explained what I needed to do. He said that it was all about trust. To get the guys to do what you want, they have to believe that you want what is best for them and the troop. Your needs come last.

They have to know that you have a plan and that they have an important part in achieving it. They must know clearly what you expect of them, and you must be sure that they know how to do it. If they don't, it is your responsibility to teach them. You also have to step up to the guys who are not doing their fair share. Everybody will be watching. Treat them with respect, but be clear about what the expectations are. Even more important, when one of the guys does something well—especially if they took initiative—recognize it and thank them for their contribution. None of this will be possible if they do not trust you. Trust must be earned over time.

Seymour explained that trust was like a bank account, and you have to keep making deposits if you want it to grow. Sometimes things will go wrong, and you will have to make a withdrawal. Meanwhile, it is sitting in the account earning interest. The greater the amount of trust in the account, the better the guys will respond. A low or negative balance of trust and you just won't be successful.

Seymour's leadership rules made tremendous sense to me. While his insights were not especially original, they were very authentic because he was a living example of them in action. I have tried to follow his advice to this day.

Mike Gannon also created his own checklist for building a strong team, which he shared with us here. It might be helpful to you as you build your own team (Figure 8.2).

Questions to Consider

- When have you been part of a particularly effective team, and what made it effective?
- What resources can you find to help you become a better listener?
- What can you do right now to improve the level of trust within your primary team and how it functions?

Figure 8.2 Mike Gannon's Team-Building Checklist

Notes

1. Katzenbach, J. R., & Smith, D. K. (1992). *The wisdom of teams: Creating the high-performance organization.* Harvard Business School Press.
2. Sundstrom, E., DeMeuse, K. P., & Futrell, D. (1990). Work teams: Applications and effectiveness. *American*, 45(2), 120–133.
3. Mathieu, J., Maynard, M. T., Rapp, T., & Gilson, L. (2008). Team effectiveness 1997–2007: A review of recent advancements and a glimpse into the future. *Journal of Management*, 34(3), 410–476.
4. Argote, L., & McGrath, J. E. (1993). Group process in organization: Continuity and change. In C. I. Cooper, & I. T. Robertson (Eds.), *International review of industrial and organizational psychology* (Vol. 8, pp. 333–389). John Wiley.
5. Goodman, P. S. (1986). The impact of task and technology on group performance. In P. Goodman & Associates (Eds), *Designing effective work groups* (pp. 120–167). Jossey-Bass.

6. Roy, I., Hauptmann, M., & Van Durme, Y. (2019, April 11). *Organizational performance: It's a team sport: 2019 global human capital trends*. Deloitte Insights. https://www2.deloitte.com/us/en/insights/focus/human-capital-trends/2019/team-based-organization.html

7. Barrick, M. B., Bradley, B. H., Kristof-Brown, A. L., & Colbert, A. E. (2007). The moderating role of top management team interdependence: Implications of real teams and working groups. *Academy of Management Journal, 50*(3), 544–557.

8. Roy, I., Hauptmann, M., & Van Durme, Y. (2019, April 11). *Organizational performance: It's a team sport: 2019 global human capital trends*. Deloitte Insights. https://www2.deloitte.com/us/en/insights/focus/human-capital-trends/2019/team-based-organization.html

9. Quinteiro, P. M., Passos, A., & Curral, L. (2016). Thought self-leadership and effectiveness in self-management teams. *Leadership, 12*(1), 110–126.

10. Hackman, J. R. (2011). *Collaborative intelligence: Using teams to solve hard problems*. Berrett-Koehler Publishers.

11. Hackman, J. R. (2011). *Collaborative intelligence: Using teams to solve hard problems*. Berrett-Koehler Publishers.

12. Mishra, A. K., & Mishra, K. E. (2013). *Becoming a trustworthy leader: Psychology and practice*. Routledge.

13. Mathieu, J., Maynard, M. T., Rapp, T., & Gilson, L. (2008). Team effectiveness 1997–2007: A review of recent advancements and a glimpse into the future. *Journal of Management, 34*(3), 410–476.

14. D'Innocenzo, L., Mathieu, J. E., & Kukenberger, M. R. (2016). A meta-analysis of different forms of shared leadership–team performance relations. *Journal of Management, 42*(7), 1964–1991.

15. Zaccaro, S. J., Rittman, A. L., & Marks, M. A. (2001). Team leadership. *The Leadership Quarterly, 12*(4), 451–483.

16. D'Innocenzo, L., Mathieu, J. E., & Kukenberger, M. R. (2016). A meta-analysis of different forms of shared leadership–team performance relations. *Journal of Management, 42*(7), 1964–1991.

17. Mishra, A. K., Isaeva, N., Mishra, K. E., and Grubb, L. K. Top management teams and response to organizational crisis: The roles of trust, power, and control. Paper presented at the *Journal of Management Studies* Special Issue on Control and Trust Dynamics Paper Workshop (online), April 29–30.

18. Ross, J. A. (2008, February 27). *Trust makes the team go 'round*. Harvard Business Review. https://hbr.org/2008/02/trust-makes-the-team-go-round-1

19. Spreitzer, G. M., Noble, D. S., Mishra, A. K., & Cooke, W. N. (1999). Predicting process improvement team performance in an automotive firm: Explicating the roles of trust and empowerment. In R. Wageman (Ed.), *Research on managing groups and team: Groups in context* (Vol. 2, pp. 71–92). JAI.

20. De Jong, B. A., & Elfring, T. (2010). How does trust affect the performance of ongoing teams? The mediating role of reflexivity, monitoring, and effort. *Academy of Management Journal, 53*(3), 535–549.

21. Penteli, N., & Tucker, R. (2009). Power and trust in global virtual teams. *Communications of the Association for Computing Machinery, 52*(12), 113–115.

22. Katzenbach, J. R., & Smith, D. K. (1992). *The wisdom of teams: Creating the high-performance organization*. Harvard Business School Press.

23. Field, A. (2006, August). Are you rewarding solo performance at the team's expense? *Harvard Management Update*, 3–5.

24. Gibson, C. B., & Cohen, S. G. (2003). *Virtual teams that work: Creating conditions for virtual team effectiveness* (p. 73). Jossey-Bass.
25. Pellathy, D. A., Mollenkopf, D. A., Stank, T. P., & Autry, C. W. (2019). Cross-functional integration: concept clarification and scale development. *Journal of Business Logistics, 40*(2), 81–104.
26. Colquitt, J. A., LePine, J. A., Zapata, C. P., & Wild, R. E. (2011). Trust in typical and high-reliability contexts: Building and reacting to trust among firefighters. *The Academy of Management Journal, 54*(5), 999–1015.
27. De Jong, B. A., & Elfring, T. (2010). How does trust affect the performance of ongoing teams? The mediating role of reflexivity monitoring, and effort. *The Academy of Management Journal, 53*(3), 535–549.
28. Langfred, C. W. (2004). Too much of a good thing? Negative effects of high trust and individual autonomy in self-managing teams. *The Academy of Management Journal, 47*(3), 385–399.
29. Langfred, C. W. (2007). The downside of self-management: A longitudinal study of the effects of conflict on trust, autonomy, and task interdependence in self-managing teams. *The Academy of Management Journal, 50*(4), 885–900.
30. Ross, J. A. (2008, February 27). *Trust makes the team go 'round.* Harvard Business Review. https://hbr.org/2008/02/trust-makes-the-team-go-round-1
31. Lau, D., & Liden, R. C. (2008). Antecedents of coworker trust: Leaders' blessings. *Journal of Applied Psychology, 93*(50), 1130–1138.
32. Schaubroeck, J., Lam, S. S. K., & Peng, A. C. (2011). Cognition-based and affect-based trust as mediators of leader behavior influences on team performance. *Journal of Applied Psychology, 96*(4), 863.

9 WHY **TEAMS** NEED **GREAT** LEADERSHIP

By the end of Bob's first year at General Motors (GM), six of the nine new college graduates who had been hired to be first-line supervisors had quit, but Bob continued to stick it out. The machine repairman who had been loafing in his cubbyhole was now always on the job, doing preventive maintenance. Things no longer broke down as often, which meant he spent less time on repair work. For Bob, the positive changes accelerated. His attitude was that whereas he knew little, his employees knew everything:

> As I got more settled into my responsibilities, I started to see some of the people who worked for me genuinely trying to help me. They saw in me someone who was generally trying to help them in a manner that respected their skills, rather than threatened them. This was just not typical of their previous experience.
>
> There were little things that showed me they viewed me as a different kind of boss. During my first year, I remember my hourly people somehow found out about my birthday, and at lunch break they had a cake. I had started in June, and my birthday was February 15th. They were glad that I was their supervisor, and they were really coming around.
>
> After things started going well, of course, then they'd move me someplace else and I'd have to start all over again, but that was because management saw we were doing some wonderful things. They continued to move me into other positions, and within three years they promoted me to a general foreman (general supervisor), where I had even more responsibility.

To be intentional as a team leader, you may need to be proactive by requesting training for yourself on how to lead the team. Such training has been shown to improve team performance.[1] More specifically, leadership training focused on improving communication skills, including empathic listening, and asking good questions, has also been shown to improve the quality of team decisions.[2]

Research shows that leaders who encourage knowledge sharing among their team contribute to team trust and better performance.[3] As team members trust each other, they begin to share even more information. The leader

 DOI: 10.4324/9780367822170-12

should be the one to trust first, in order to set an example for others to trust as well.

Ariel Investments co-CEO John Rogers Jr. shared his perspective on teamwork:

> My basketball coach at Princeton, Pete Carril, changed my life. He taught me the importance of teamwork first and foremost, and that to be successful you had to think about your teammates first.

Research has also shown that a team leader's EQ "is significantly related to the presence of emotionally competent group norms on the teams they lead, and that emotionally competent group norms are related to team performance."[4] Trust researcher Kurt Dirks also found that trust in the leader has a direct, positive effect on team performance.[5] This trust in the leader allows followers to accept their role, embrace the mission of the organization, and perform well.

Our former Wake Forest University colleague Kellie Sauls shared how she built trust with her team:

> I led a team that encompassed smaller teams tasked with integral parts of the client's full experience and journey. Each team understood their part in the overall experience, and we communicated everything consistently. We all were different and were respected. We liked one another, and we all did really good work. We had fun doing it.

Proactive (or intentional) leaders enhance team performance because transitioning into a new team leadership role requires the leader to set goals and convince the team to achieve them.[6] Karen's MBA student Daniel Quinn shared his experience creating an excellent team during his deployment:

> The last team I served with in Iraq and Afghanistan was very special. It was right before the drawdown in Iraq, and things were crazy. My department had been gutted, with everyone having been sent back to the States. It was then that I realized my group still had a very key mission, and we needed to get to work. With limited resources and personnel, I just threw together a team consisting of all branches, including someone from the Coast Guard. We had never worked together before, had limited equipment, minimal support, and a major task to complete.
>
> We all came together and worked on combining our strengths and overcoming our weaknesses. We had the most successful six-month period in the history of the International Military Education and Training,[7] per General Lloyd Austin.

Setting agendas is a key part of effective goal setting, even for relatively simple teams. As our GM boss Mike Gannon shared:

> When I was in elementary school, I was a Cub Scout, and my mom was the leader of our den. Our den was comprised of about eight boys that were in my grade in school. We met every Tuesday after school to work on projects and earn achievements towards various advancements and awards. My mom—who was a teacher—was always very well prepared with a detailed lesson plan. As a result, we always had fun and accomplished a lot during her meetings. I thought it looked pretty easy.
>
> When I graduated to the Boy Scouts, all the boys in my Cub Scout den also joined and we formed the Flaming Arrow Patrol. The patrols—like Cub Scout dens—were supposed to meet after school and work on projects and advancements. The big difference was that we did not have an adult leader. The patrol leader (elected by the boys) was responsible for planning and leading the patrol meeting.
>
> I was elected the patrol leader and looked forward to running my first meeting. Of course, I didn't have any plan for the meeting and did not make any preparations. I was shocked and crushed that the meeting was a miserable disaster. At dinner that night, I was moping and sighing, and my parents asked what was wrong. I explained about my horrible meeting.
>
> My mom asked me if I had made a plan for the meeting. What? Why would I do that? She explained the preparation she had done for our Cub Scout meetings, and it was like a revelation. I had no idea! So, my mom helped me make a standard plan for future meetings with things like the purpose of the meeting, who should bring the treats, what game we were going to play, what was going to be our activity, and what materials I needed to prepare in advance.
>
> My next patrol meeting was a great success, and I recall how pleased I was when one of my friends said it was "the best meeting ever." To this day, thanks to this early lesson from my mom, I never have a meeting without a purpose, a plan, and an agenda. I learned early on that it was a basic building block to demonstrating competence and trust as a leader.

It almost sounds trite to say that trust and effective teams go together. Nevertheless, especially when people are highly vulnerable, trust must form if the team is to function. Our friend Joe Wilcox, a military veteran and Karen's former MBA student, described his experience building high-trust teams in a high-stakes environment:

> In 2013, I was deployed to Helmand province, Afghanistan. I worked on a multinational team of four British K-9 handlers (the dogs were

Brits too), one Norwegian, 10 US Marines, and two Afghan inter-preters. Our team developed a close bond, and what I think made that happen was being in a high-stakes environment. I believe this applies to other industries where the stakes are high, too, not just the military.

Trust and empowerment also go hand in hand, as our own research demon-strates. Team leaders who trust their team members will be more likely to delegate authority to them, while providing support as needed. Karen's MBA student Joe Wilcox described the best team he worked on during his active-duty service:

> The best team that I ever worked on was during my active-duty service with the United States Marines. I was assigned to a very high-visibility project that was being sponsored by the Marines' senior-ranking uni-formed officer. There was a tremendous amount of pressure to deliver, but the individual leading our team never let this affect his leadership style. He exhibited a very calm, consistent behavior throughout the 18-month project, regardless of what was happening.
>
> His leadership style was to make sure that the team knew what they needed to accomplish and then let us work and manage our portions of the project. He didn't micromanage or interfere but was always available for support and guidance. When we ran into issues, his approach was always to spend time understanding what happened and then focus on how best to move forward—no finger-pointing or blaming. It was a great learning experience for me, and I have tried to incorporate these elements into my own leadership ever since.

Authentic leaders improve team performance because their self-control improves task-related team processes. But self-control does not mean denying one's emotions. Displaying emotional vulnerability can actually build trust. Jenny Meyer, energy industry consultant, describes how her team has bonded over their individual vulnerabilities:

> They know that 'I have their backs' and we have built a culture that promotes authenticity. I know I am "safe" with my team—I can be vulnerable. During one of our first assignments, we sat on the countertop in a conference room in tears talking about our deceased sons. One of my guys had lost his wife to a brutal battle with cancer in the same year I had lost my son. Tragedy brought my team together because we can share our stories. Tragedy can be an amazing catalyst. You can use it as a catapult to do great things. The truly awesome thing about my team is that they are all pas-sionate about helping industry avoid incidents and save lives. We all have a shared passion for helping people.

Questions to Consider

- Who is the best leader you have ever worked for, and what did you learn from them?
- Whether you want to lead a team, or are already leading one, what leadership training (or other resources) do you need from your boss right now?
- How can you set the example for your team, to share information and trust first?

Notes

1. Santos, J. P., Caetano, A., & Tavares, S. M. (2015). Is training leaders in functional leadership a useful tool for improving the performance of leadership functions and team effectiveness? *The Leadership Quarterly*, 26(3), 470–484.
2. Meyer, B., Burtscher, M. J., Jonas, K., Feese, S., Arnrich, B., Tröster, G., & Schermuly, C. C. (2016). What good leaders actually do: Micro-level leadership behaviour, leader evaluations, and team decision quality. *European Journal of Work and Organizational Psychology*, 25(6), 773–789.
3. Lee, P., Gillespie, N., Mann, L., & Wearing, A. (2010). Leadership and trust: Their effect on knowledge sharing and team performance. *Management Learning*, 41(4), 473–491.
4. Koman, E. S., & Wolff, S. B. (2008). Emotional intelligence competencies in the team and team leader: A multi-level examination of the impact of emotional intelligence on team performance. *Journal of Management Development*, 27(1), 55–75.
5. Dirks, K. T. (2000). Trust in leadership and team performance: Evidence from NCAA basketball. *Journal of Applied Psychology*, 85(6), 1004–1012.
6. Lam, W., Lee, C., Taylor, M. S., & Zhao, H. H. (2018). Does proactive personality matter in leadership transitions? Effects of proactive personality on new leader identification and responses to new leaders and their change agendas. *Academy of Management Journal*, 61(1), 245–263.
7. IMET, or International Military Education and Training, is a program to enhance regional stability through mutually beneficial military-to-military relations. Wikipedia. https://en.wikipedia.org/wiki/International_Military_Education_and_Training

10
BUILD THE RIGHT TEAM WITH WHO YOU HAVE

For one of his teams, Bob inherited a personnel director, a well-educated man, who clearly did not want to work constructively with the local UAW. For several years, he had resisted Bob's efforts to build trust and collaborate with the union. His antagonistic approach culminated with his negotiations with the union over installing drinking fountains throughout the plant, something the union had wanted for years. On the day that the fountains were installed, the head of the union turned one on as part of the unveiling ceremony, only to have no water come out. The personnel director quipped, "You asked for drinking fountains, but you didn't ask for the plumbing to bring water to them." Bob was sick of this all-too typical gamesmanship of this man. Bob had drawn a line in the sand regarding this manager's behavior with respect to the union, and now the personnel director had crossed it. Bob then worked with GM's corporate headquarters staff to replace him, someone who would be willing to contribute to Bob's effort to change the culture of the plant.

Intentionally leading teams begins with selecting the right people to be on the team. As John Rogers Jr., co-CEO of Ariel Investments, put it:

> You surround yourself with people who are competent in their ability, and competent in challenging the leader. To be successful, you always want to surround yourself with the strongest, most dynamic people.

Brooke Wilson, Two Men and a Truck franchisee, shared how she hires people for her team:

> When recruiting members to my team, I look for ownership and work ethic. All team players must "own" their role and take pride in delivering successfully. They must be supportive of the team, and willing to take direction. Job skills and knowledge can be trained, but work ethic and a sense of accountability are often nurtured behaviors derived from formative experiences. It's hard to make someone different in this regard.

> Building a team starts with assessing the project need. What skills are required to complete the project successfully, how many team members are allowed in the budget? Then, I start meeting and

DOI: 10.4324/9780367822170-13

interviewing people. It's important that each player balances the strengths and weaknesses within the team.

Intentionally leading teams means developing norms, rules, and guidelines for team behavior that reinforce the ROCC of Trust. Aneil's college classmate Hal Stern shared how he empowers his team:

> Building trust with others is the complement to empowerment. I will empower teams to design, deliver, and lead if we share the same trust framework—the same set of ordered priorities that determine how good business and personal outcomes are measured. When you run into the cases where you need to say "no" or "we need more information" or "how does this fit into the larger picture," then it's easier to lead because you trust your team to have the difficult conversations. The corollary is that if I empower my teams, they must trust me to back them in those difficult conversations—when they say "no" to a project or idea or insist on changing a team structure.

Mike Gannon, our former GM boss, agreed that having the right people on the team sends an important message:

> I have found that getting the leadership team right is essential to establishing a team that is built on trust. The type of performance and behavior that you tolerate, the type of people that you reward with promotions, and the level of talent that you recruit from the outside will tell your team if you are a reliable and competent leader.

Intentional leaders also put people into positions on a team based on their strengths. Dr. Anitra Manning of IBM shared that she has been graced with the gift of discerning the strengths and talents of those that she is working with and how to best deploy them. She believes that when the right people are in the right place, the team is effective but so is that individual. She believes that healthy families and communities are shaped in the workplace.

> I started to cultivate the gift of caring influence when I was in high school. Since then, I have honed it within undergraduate and graduate organizations, workplaces, and community organizations. While I've read and written the curriculum of several leadership development programs over the years, I learned the most by watching women in educational, faith, and familial environments. But I also love to watch people. I also like to ask a lot of questions so that I get to know people. Some might say that I am a bit nosy (I like to call it learned powerful observation and I proudly learned it from my grandparents who were the mayors of their block in Brooklyn,

New York). I have watched what motivates and demotivates others and have used those insights to redesign conditions so that people want to offer their best selves to the work. I have learned that authenticity yields productivity. Every time that I have led—from high school, college, and in my current work, I get to know the people on the team, talk with them about their perceived/untapped strengths, and regularly solicit their critical support. We can never take a previous "yes" for granted. Leaders must constantly secure commitment. I also use the distributed model that I saw as a child. Whenever I am leading or can exercise influence, I invite the team to match project tasks with individual skills and personal strengths. This caring influence model has matured with time as I continue to grow as an adaptive, inclusive, and people-agile leader.

Professor Ron Riggio is a leadership scholar who also studies followership, or the nature and impact of followers and following in the leadership process.[1] We, ourselves, like to think that the purpose of mentoring followers is to develop them into future leaders. When leaders and followers trust each other, work is collaborative, people are engaged, communication is effective, and people care about each other. Rick Warren describes the process of moving from follower to leader as "passing the baton": first we learn from a "mentor," then we have a "pacesetter" to look up to, and finally we collaborate with our "partner" or colleague as an equal.[2] This is a positive way to look at both our own growth as a leader as well as how we can mentor other employees as they grow into their own leadership. Aneil's former colleague Steve Fitzgerald described the way in which we might be both leader and follower:

> I have become absolutely convinced that the traits of really good followership and strong leadership are not all that different, and that good leaders often are bouncing back and forth between the roles. At the end of the day, leaders who lead well make choices that benefit the greater good. They understand the goal; they understand the charter that they're out to achieve. They put aside both their personal aspirations and their needs, as well as some of their wants, and they make choices that are aligned with the goals, the charter, and the stakeholders. That's a really good description of good followership, too.

> Likewise, good leaders and good followers are both vocal when they are experiencing dissonance between those goals or the charter. They speak truth to power. For followers, that means communicating it up the hierarchy. For leaders, that can mean being willing to confront the poor behavior or misalignment of your followers' behavior. There are plenty of leaders who struggle with that.

Aneil's former WFU Dean Charlie Moyer described his method for sharing leadership in order to maximize decision-making:

> When I agreed to become the dean, I reached out to my colleague, Chuck, and I said, "I want you to be my associate dean." He said, "We don't agree on much," to which I replied, "That's why I want you to be my associate dean. There's a promise I'll make to you: I will never make an important decision without having a full discussion of it. Sometimes you'll change my mind, and sometimes I hope I'll change your mind, but at the end of the day the only thing I ask is that once we've decided, after you and I fully work it out, that you support it." He agreed to do that.

LEADER AGILITY

A growing number of leadership scholars and practitioners are now focusing on the importance of leadership agility and its beneficial impact on organizational learning, innovation, and other outcomes. Kevin Cashman of Korn Ferry describes the importance of leaders who possess leadership agility, or the ability to "toggle mental, interpersonal, and results-focused approaches towards accomplishment and advancement."[3] Leadership agility includes the ability to step back and see the big picture, the ability to focus on key stakeholders and have empathy for their perspective, the ability to reflect on one's own leadership strengths, and the ability to be innovative in the face of challenges and obstacles.[4] The agility that leaders can foster in their followers is also important. As our GM mentor Mike Gannon told us:

> We exist in a time when change comes at us at a very rapid rate. To be successful, both individuals and teams must now become experts in adapting to change quickly. Adapting quickly to change requires that each person continually expand their mindset or mental model. Changing your mindset means changing the things that influence your viewpoint. It also means getting out of your comfort zone. While people (say that they) hate change, what they fear are the transitions caused by change.
>
> One of my favorite analogies about the change process and transitions is the trapeze act at the circus. As part of this act, the performer must let go of one trapeze and fly through the air and trust that the next trapeze will be perfectly positioned for them to grab hold of and reach the other side. If the person sending the second trapeze doesn't perfectly time their throw, the performer will not make the "transition" and will fall to the ground.
>
> In the change process, an employee must let go of their comfort zone, make a leap of faith, and trust that the new opportunity will be there to grab ahold of. A leader can use the analogy of trapeze

artists in a circus to explain the physics of how the "second trapeze" will be in the right place for them to catch, the benefits of getting to the other side, and the reasons why they can't stay where they are, but employees may still be reluctant to make a change. This will be especially true if the employees do not trust what they are being told about the situation or trust that the second trapeze will be waiting for them at the right time.

Now imagine the situation where the leader has established a long relationship of trust with those employees who need to make the change and transition to a new place. As a result, the employees will believe their leader once they have explained the situation and provided information and ideas about the future. They will also appreciate that their leader can share their own concerns and be compassionate about the employees' fears. They can watch as their leader swings from one trapeze to the other and makes the transition to the other side. As a result, employees will trust that their leader will perfectly position the second trapeze to allow them to transition to the other side.

Of course, any first change process and transition will be difficult for the team. But as the team gains more trust in the process, the next change process will be easier to manage. Soon, like trapeze artists in the circus, they will more easily swing—still with some fear—from one trapeze to another. I believe that is the model for establishing agility in an organization, and trust is the foundation for that to happen.

Once you have put your team together, then you need to think about building the right team culture to retain your team members and get them to perform optimally, which means trust-based coaching. As John Rogers Jr. of Ariel Investments told us:

> I was fortunate to work at William Blair & Company. The culture of William Blair was able to recruit people and keep them for the long term. I think, as a leader, it's important to have the perspective that you're going to try to find a way to keep your teammates on the team.

Questions to Consider

- What three norms would be the most important for your current or future team?
- Think about a team you belong to now: What would you say is the primary goal or purpose of your team?
- If you are the leader of a team, what do you need to do to create a greater commitment to that goal or purpose?

Notes

1. Riggio, R. E. (2014). Followership research: Looking back and looking forward. *Journal of Leadership Education, 13*(4), 15-20.
2. Warren, R. (2014, February 6). *3 phases of a Paul and Timothy relationship.* Pastors. com. https://pastors.com/paul-timothy/
3. Cashman, K. (2008). Leader agility. *Leadership Excellence, 20.*
4. Joiner, B. (2019). Leadership agility for organizational agility. *Journal of Creating Value, 5*(2), 139–149.

11

THE **TEAM** LEADER **IS** A **TRUSTED** COACH

After Bob had made the decision to remain with GM, he eventually was moved to the Chevy plant's group responsible for quality improvement. Bob and his colleagues were all working on the plant's first shift. Typically, at the end of the shift, the manager in charge would bring all his people into his office, even though it was time to go home. Bob recalls:

> Then he'd tell us what dummies we all were because we weren't hitting our quality measures. We'd have to sit there and listen to how "Charlie" screwed up before he told you how you screwed up. My wife, Karen, and I only had one car at the time, and she would be in the car waiting to pick me up. Sometimes she had to wait an hour. Sometimes it was two hours while he rattled on about our ineffectiveness. Maybe he saw his approach as constructive, but it simply wasn't because of his demeanor, his tone of voice, his timing, and because he criticized us in front of each other.

In contrast, the Bob's next top boss at the Chevy plant, Jay Wisner, deeply appreciated what the young college-graduate supervisors had to offer. An outgoing, relatively young manager, he mentored Bob and his fellow graduates leading on the shop floor by helping them learn to navigate the treacherous culture they worked in, while also working with them to improve that culture. Bob remembers him fondly: "He really helped my career on three or four occasions, making recommendations to other top management people that maybe I had something special to offer."

Once you are leading a team, you will want to be *intentional* about developing them. As Aneil's former colleague Steve Fitzgerald told us:

> Really good leaders are very comfortable delegating to trusted subordinates, even trusting them to make really important choices, because that person has become immersed in a topic that the leader is not.

Research shows that the leader has the important role of building trust within a team,[1] particularly when teams are new and team members have no history with one another. As John Rogers Jr. of Ariel Investments said:

DOI: 10.4324/9780367822170-14

I like to say it's how you treat people. You can tell when people are listening to you versus when they're going through the motions. I think when you're trying to create an environment of trust, you've got to tell people right up front, "I want to hear what's on your mind," and then show that you're really listening to them.

Anita Johnson shared how she develops her team:

Provide assignments that challenge their thinking and stretch them. Don't let the team member return the task to you if they find it difficult. It's okay if they struggle a bit. Let them understand you have confidence in their abilities. Give candid and constructive feedback, supported by recognition. Communicate your awareness of their development. Provide feedback on an ongoing basis, so there are no surprises when it comes time for a formal performance evaluation.

Teams that are new develop by having clear, measurable and common objectives, a culture set by the leader that values listening, diverse input and "fun" while getting the tasks accomplished and recognition between and among the team members and leader.

In employee surveys, the number one preferred leadership method identified is coaching.[2] Coaching is a positive way to encourage employees, helping them to understand their strengths and reach their potential. As the leader, you could coach your employees individually or in teams. Team coaching is defined as "direct interaction with a team intended to help members make coordinated and task-appropriate use of their collective resources in accomplishing the team's work."[3]

As a coach, the leader is responsible for helping the team identify team problems and consulting with the team about issues surrounding team processes and team problem-solving.[4] Evidence has shown that a leader's team coaching leads to improved team satisfaction, empowerment, and improved relationships among team members.[5] Like the coach of a sports team, the leader can fill an important role in helping their team reach its full potential. Still, it is important for leaders to inform their team members about how they plan to develop them, or risk being accused of favoritism. TASCO vice president Jim McCown shared the challenges of building a team in a global environment:

When I moved to Mexico, it was to take over the VP [vice president] role in charge of the team of which I had previously been a member. I knew the team well and knew where I needed to focus my energies. I had eight directors and purposely did not spend the same amount of time with each of them, and instead based it on greatest needs in my first six months. My director in charge of merchandising analysis came to see me one day, and very honestly asked if there was a problem. He had been wondering why I just didn't seem to spend that much time with him.

It caught me by surprise, and we had a great talk. I explained that I had eight direct reports plus my administrative assistant. I further explained that he had my implicit trust and that the message I had intended by essentially leaving him alone was that he was doing a great job. My personal preference is to be left alone, so I would have loved it. He needed, however, to be told what was happening. That was a big learning moment for me that I took to my next company, Canadian Tire, and leveraged each time I had a new director join my team.

Mentoring and coaching, rather than supervising and directing, were Mike Gannon's preferred approaches to managing the work of his subordinates. This approach also built trust, as monitoring or micromanaging impairs trust with followers.[6] Neither of us can recall being told how to perform any of our tasks, unless we specifically asked Mike. His approach was to let us figure out the best way to do them and ask for help when needed. We might even go an entire day or more without interacting with Mike other than to say, "good morning" or "have a nice evening." At the time, we thought that this was the way leaders and managers typically acted, not having had many bosses before we worked for Mike. In more than three and a half decades since we both worked for him; however, we have learned that his approach to managing and leading is rare, especially when considering that we worked for him in the early 1980s.

Mike shared with us his more recent approach to coaching his employees. He described his role as making every member of the team accountable to realize the vision:

Once the HR vision was well understood, I established annual HR priorities that would help move the HR function towards realizing our statement of purpose. As part of that process, every member of the global HR team had to commit to a personal objective that supported the HR priorities for the year. The proposed objectives were submitted to me for approval and once approved, each team member was personally accountable to me for achieving their objective. Obviously, a clerk might have a much different objective than an executive, but the point was to ensure each team member could clearly see the alignment between the priorities of the HR function and what they were working on.

They submitted written progress reports to me quarterly, but at least once per year, and usually twice, the report was made to me personally during one of my site review meetings. Employees had love–hate feelings about the process. Many of them hated having to give presentations to "Mike" because they normally did not have to do that sort of thing. But on the other hand, most began to enjoy the process as they came to understand that it was really a coaching session and a chance to share work that they were proud of accomplishing. It was also a chance for the team to understand that Mike was a real person that they could easily talk too.

Being an agile leader in terms of adjusting one's coaching style is also critical. Chris Deshazor of Harness described how his approach to leading has changed over time:

> I am not a micromanager. If you need something, you just let me know. You have a job to do. You know what you're supposed to do. I have a job to do, I know what I'm supposed to do. If you need me, you call me. I have my trusted Verizon flip phone. Call me on my flip and we're good.

> But, over the years, I've totally done a 180 because my training in situational leadership and my evolution as a leader based on listening made it clear to me that there are people who sometimes need more guidance. When they need more guidance, you need to be there for them.

> As an example, my boss gave a project to my direct report. During my weekly catchups, I noticed she wasn't mentioning the project. I asked, "What's going on?" She responded with some general information, but no specifics. Then, in my meeting with my boss, he asked about the project because he was concerned that it was really slowing down.

> I went back to her and found out she'd been struggling with the project and procrastinating as a result. I totally changed my leadership approach and became more direct, more involved. I started asking very pointed questions. I literally micromanaged her, and watched her go from "I don't know" to "thank you." Later on, she told me, "I'm so glad you did that because I was struggling. I didn't know how to say that. I was getting pressured about getting this done and I just didn't want to fail. I was doing whatever I thought was right, and what I thought was right, was actually wrong."

Questions to Consider

- How has a stretch assignment improved your capabilities?
- How does your boss act like a coach right now?
- What do you need to do to be a better coach?

Notes

1. Ross, J. A. (2005, November). Team camaraderie: Can you have too much? *Harvard Management Update*, 3–4.
2. Indeed. (2021, December 8). *10 common leadership styles (plus how to find your own)*. https://www.indeed.com/career-advice/career-development/10-common-leadership-styles
3. Hackman, J. R. & Wageman, R. (2005). A theory of team coaching. *Academy of Management Review, 30*(2), 269–287.
4. Mathieu, J., Maynard, M. T., Rapp, T., & Gilson, L. (2008). Team effectiveness 1997–2007: A review of recent advancements and a glimpse into the future. *Journal of Management, 34*(3), 410–476.
5. Mathieu, J., Maynard, M. T., Rapp, T., & Gilson, L. (2008). Team effectiveness 1997–2007: A review of recent advancements and a glimpse into the future. *Journal of Management, 34*(3), 410–476.
6. Robison, J. (2020, January 17). *Give up bossing, take up coaching: You'll like the results*. Gallup. https://www.gallup.com/workplace/282647/give-bossing-coaching-results.aspx

12 ENGAGE **AND** EMPOWER **REMOTE** TEAMS

Before there was remote work as we know it today, Bob would provide quarterly business updates to all employees, in person. To accomplish this, it meant spending two to three days holding 35-plus meetings across all three shifts, which was very hard to do, yet Bob still felt he should be communicating more frequently with the thousands of employees who worked for him. Consequently, he promoted Dave Nedrich to fill the new position of communications coordinator. Dave began producing weekly videos lasting 10–15 minutes of Bob communicating key information and goals for the plant. Each work team would watch the video during their weekly meetings and apply it to their own tasks and objectives. Thus began, *Video Bob*. Even then, Bob had the task of ensuring that all employees, no matter when or where they worked, felt like they were all on the same team.

Dave then came up with the idea of doing interviews with people on the floor to see how they felt about their organization. These interviews did not take place every week, but at least monthly, they would choose an hourly employee at random and ask them a question regarding their work, how they liked it, how they viewed the changes that were taking place, and whether they saw the plant as changing for the better.

On one occasion, when asked if the plant was improving, an employee responded, "That's a bunch of b.s. I hate this place. It's no different at all." Dave tried to find out more asking, "You don't see any improvement at all?" The guy paused, looked directly at Dave, and said, "No, that's not really true. There has been a big change. In fact, I don't hate this place at all. I love coming to work now." Then he added, "Now that I think about it, I haven't told my wife I love her in 30 years. When I go home tonight, I'm going to tell her I love her." In reflecting on the employee's comments, Bob said, "People felt that it was not in vogue to be positive. They had grown up in a culture where everybody hated everybody."

In his approach to two-way communication, Bob was a pioneering internal communicator. He knew the power of sharing important information with employees first before they learned about it from someone else. It also helped him and his leadership team to build trust, loyalty, and respect among the employees.

Remote teams should be anything but remote when it comes to working closely. Even before COVID-19, more and more teams were working together virtually from various locations, either in the same state or from around the

DOI: 10.4324/9780367822170-15

world. For example, a recent survey of 1,372 business respondents from 80 countries found that 85% of the respondents worked in virtual teams and 48% reported that over half their virtual team members were members of other cultures.[1]

One study found that before COVID-19, only 17% of employees worked remotely each week.[2] Now, due to COVID-19, 44% of employees report working from home.[3] As of December 2020, most workers who said their job responsibilities can mainly be done from home said that before the pandemic, they rarely or never teleworked. Before the pandemic, 20% said they worked from home all or most of the time, but during the pandemic, 71% were doing their job from home all or most of the time.[4] This trend is not likely to return to the way it was now that employees are seeing the benefits of flexibility and employers are enjoying lower real estate costs. Samantha Pittman, Aneil's former East Carolina University (ECU) graduate assistant and now an Assistant VP for Robert Half, shared her experience of improved communication with remote teams:

> Effective remote teams require overcommunication. I find it is most helpful to have a chat dedicated to work and a chat dedicated to anything outside of work. Sometimes it's also fun to throw a meeting onto the Teams calendar to discuss the weekend or how things are going instead of the same typical business agenda.

Previous research has shown that leadership behavior is very important to trust and commitment within virtual teams.[5] One study found that having a shared vision, such as a customer focus, rather than emphasizing who has the most power in the group, helped a virtual team achieve higher levels of trust.[6] This same study found that high-trust groups shared power within the group based on the knowledge that each individual brought to the group. Finally, those high-trust groups functioned well if they had a facilitator who reinforced and encouraged the shared vision. Another study has shown that relational building efforts, including trust-building, enhance team innovation in a virtual work environment.[7] One of our former students shared their recent experience with remote work:

> Effective remote teams require allowing people flexibility in terms of the hours they work as long as they get the job done. Having a weekly meeting on Monday so the team can discuss what they worked on the previous week and what they plan to work on this week. Having virtual or in-person happy hours once a quarter are also effective.

The extent to which members contribute to conversations or share knowledge with each other contributes to trust within virtual teams.[8] In addition, when virtual team members stick to deadlines, they are considered more trustworthy because they demonstrate their reliability.[9] Joe Wilcox,

Karen's former MBA student, shared what works in his current remote work environment:

> Communication and knowing what the plan is and staying on schedule. I believe employing Gantt charts and backward planning help keep a virtual team humming. Work is different in a virtual environment, so learning how to plan backward, and really learning what is due when is a must.

It is also important for leaders of teams to build trust among themselves as they lead their teams in these new environments. Chris Deshazor, talent management executive at Harness, has found that he can help other leaders in the organization find a safe place to share their challenges:

> We do manager round tables. It's a place where managers have a safe place to come and talk about what's going on with their teams for an hour. We'll have a set topic for the month, but managers are also just talking about their teams.

Questions to Consider

- How do you keep the channels of communication open in your virtual team(s)?
- How do you continue to develop your team's strengths in a virtual environment?
- How do you show your team that you care?

Notes

1. CultureWizard, R. W. (n.d.).*RW3 Virtual Teams Survey*. Culture Wizard Virtual Teams Survey. Retrieved October 21, 2021, from https://www.rw-3.com/virtual-teams-survey-0
2. Mlitz, K. (2021, April 9). *Remote work frequency before and after COVID-19 in the United States 2020*, Statista. https://www.statista.com/statistics/1122987/change-in-remote-work-trends-after-covid-in-usa/
3. Mlitz, K. (2021, April 9). *Remote work frequency before and after COVID-19 in the United States 2020*, Statista. https://www.statista.com/statistics/1122987/change-in-remote-work-trends-after-covid-in-usa/
4. Parker, K., Menasche Horowitz, J., & Minkin, R. (2020, December 9). *How the coronavirus outbreak has – and hasn't – changed the way Americans work*. Pew Research Center. https://www.pewresearch.org/social-trends/2020/12/09/how-the-coronavirus-outbreak-has-and-hasnt-changed-the-way-americans-work/
5. Joshi, A., Lazarova, M. B., & Liao, H. (2009). Getting everyone onboard: The role of inspirational leadership in geographically dispersed teams. *Organization Science*, 20(1), 240–252.

6. Panteli, N., & Tucker, R. (2009). Power and trust in global virtual teams. *Communications of the ACM, 51*(12), 113–115.
7. Batarseh, F. S., & Usher, J. M. (2017). Collaboration capability in virtual teams: Examining the influence on diversity and innovation. *International Journal of Innovation Management, 21*(4), 1–29.
8. Panteli, N., & Tucker, R. (2009). Power and trust in global virtual teams. *Communications of the ACM, 51*(12), 113–115.
9. Panteli, N., & Tucker, R. (2009). Power and trust in global virtual teams. *Communications of the ACM, 51*(12), 113–115.

PART III

BUILDING A CULTURE OF TRUST

13

BUILDING A CULTURE OF TRUST AND WHY IT MATTERS

In this section, we discuss how organizational leaders can intentionally build a culture of trust. Using our research-based examples and across a diverse set of perspectives, we show how leaders have been able to build cultures of trust in several different sectors and industries. In times of uncertainty, it is critical to maintain (or even rebuild) a culture of trust and reinforce the values and processes that cement such a culture. Again, using our exemplars, we show how the ROCC of Trust can be built at the organizational level by being intentional. Finally, we draw upon a wide variety of leaders to help the reader understand the importance of building a diverse and inclusive organization, which will in turn enhance the trustworthiness of the leader, the team, and the organization.

Gradually, a lot of the upper levels of management started to treat Bob with a little more respect. He recalls:

> Other supervisors, traditional supervisors that came up from the ranks, were coming to me for advice. "How did you do that? How did you get those people to do that? How did you get "Charlie" out of his cubbyhole and do preventative maintenance all day?"
>
> I knew, of course, that these other supervisors who had risen through the ranks were being treated just like I was when I started. They were being threatened all the time, were afraid of losing their jobs, and they saw me being successful. So, we had a lot of side conversations behind the vending machine, with me having a cup of coffee and giving them advice.

When this happened, Bob led with the caring aspect of the ROCC of Trust. While employees were getting to know how reliable, open, honest, and competent Bob was, they first understood how much he cared for them and the plant, more so than for himself. Trustworthiness is not only saying you will do the right things but actually doing the right things.

Our General Motors (GM) mentor Mike Gannon explained the way change is perceived in organizations: "When trying to explain change to an organization, they may not say the actual words, 'Trust me' in their statements, but that is what they imply. Unfortunately, all too often people's response is: 'I don't trust you now, and I never have!'"

DOI: 10.4324/9780367822170-17

WHAT IS A CULTURE OF TRUST?

Organizational culture is revealed in the informal, implicit part of the organization that people tacitly agree upon each day through their work.[1] Culture is reinforced through the specific ways that organizational members share their vision, ideals, and values with each other.[2] Leadership and culture go hand in hand. Leadership is a result of culture, and culture is a result of leadership.[3] Our University of Michigan Ross School of Business mentors Dr. Kim Cameron and Dr. Bob Quinn in their book *Diagnosing and Changing Organizational Culture*, make the point that improving organizational culture can result in improving organizational effectiveness.[4] We highly recommend their book for greater detail and insight in how to use their Competing Values framework to diagnose and improve culture. In his book *Leading Culture Change in Global Organizations*, Dr. Dan Denison, another mentor of Aneil's, also proves how culture impacts performance in four main ways: mission and direction; adaptability and flexibility; involvement and engagement; and consistency.[5]

Aneil's college friend Hal Stern shared his own definition of culture:

> I have perhaps a strange definition of culture. I look at it as the first derivative of brain output; namely, how quickly and how well ideas spread through an organization. If you want new ideas—those that challenge the organization, that challenge the status quo—to take root, then you have to create a safe environment for those ideas. You have to give them an audience and explore them publicly. Someone once said, "[Hal] is never happy," which is only partially correct. I'm almost never content, because I feel there's always one more new idea, one more insight that will create an "Aha moment." That's probably also why I never finished writing the non-fiction book I started 20 years ago, because I am never satisfied with the thematic or plot devices.

THE BENEFITS OF A CULTURE OF TRUST

One reason for creating a culture of trust is that it is a source of competitive advantage. Trust is at an all-time low in the public's assessment of business as an institution. The most recent Edelman Trust Barometer finds that CEO credibility is at an all-time low.[6] Employees expect their employers to speak up about societal issues,[7] yet do not completely trust their employers to care about their best interests. This is not surprising given the frequency with which organizations downsize their workforces,[8] emphasize short-term profit maximization over long-term customer and employee loyalty,[9] and often only provide window dressing rather than making real efforts to be environmentally sustainable.[10] Unsurprisingly, employees are quitting at record levels to maintain their own sense of self and live out their own values.[11]

Because of the many tangible benefits that come from employees trusting their top management and one another, including a greater sense

Table 13.1 The Differences Between Organizations With and Without a Culture of Trust

Culture of Trust	Culture of Distrust
• Open communication	• Secrets
• Engagement	• Turnover
• Innovation	• Little risk taking
• Collaboration	• Competition over resources
• Ethical behavior	• Legal violations
• Higher financial performance	• Poorer financial performance
• Leaders who care about the organization more than for themselves	• Leaders who care about themselves more than for the organization

of responsibility for the organization's performance, a culture of trust has been found to enhance both sales performance and customer service.[12] Organizational innovation and long-term profitability critically depend on risk-taking, employee engagement, and productivity,[13] and the sharing of scarce resources, both across teams and the organization as a whole. The competitive advantage from these and other benefits of trustworthy cultures then results in higher levels of financial performance. Cultures of trust also promote greater legal compliance and conformity with ethical norms.[14] In our own recent research, trust within top management teams was positively related to power-sharing, cross-functional collaboration, product quality and, as a result, higher product quality and profitability.[15]

Phil Wilhelm, a cyber security expert, shared how a well-structured mission and vision statement can help him promote a trustworthy culture:

> If it is a legitimate mission or vision statement, one that people can rally behind, it gets people excited about how to pursue their jobs. Then, when I have to inevitably give them feedback, I can always point back to the North Star of our mission and vision to help them focus on why we are there.

In our research on trustworthy organizations over almost 30 years, we have found significant differences between those with cultures of trust and those without, as you see outlined in Table 13.1:

We next share how Bob Lintz and other leaders have built such cultures of trust.

Questions to Consider

- How does your organizational culture evidence trust or distrust? What would you add to our lists?
- What needs to be done to improve the culture of trust in your organization or team?
- Where can you get started?

Notes

1. Schein, E. H. (2010). *Organizational culture and leadership* (Vol. 2). John Wiley & Sons.
2. Fairholm, G. W. (1994). *Leadership and the culture of trust*. ABC-Clio/Greenwood Publishing Group.
3. Wildavsky, A. (1984). *The Nursing father: Moses as a political leader*. University of Alabama Press.
4. Cameron, K. S., & Quinn, R. E. (2011). *Diagnosing and changing organizational culture: Based on the competing values framework* (3rd ed.). John Wiley & Sons.
5. Denison, D., Hooijberg, R., Lane, N., & Lief, C. (2012). *Leading culture change in global organizations: Aligning culture and strategy* (Vol. 394, p. 2). John Wiley & Sons.
6. Edelman (n.d.). *2021 Edelman trust* barometer. https://www.edelman.com/trust/2021-trust-barometer
7. Edelman (n.d.). *2021 Edelman trust* barometer. https://www.edelman.com/trust/2021-trust-barometer
8. De Meuse, K. P. & Dai, G. (2012). Reducing costs and improving efficiency or damaging the company? In C. L. Cooper, A. Pandey, & J. C. Quick (eds), *Downsizing: Is less still more?* Cambridge University Press, pp. 258–290.
9. Ibid.
10. Ibid.
11. Hsu, A. (2021, June 24). *As the pandemic recedes, millions of workers are saying "I quit."* NPR. https://www.npr.org/2021/06/24/1007914455/as-the-pandemic-recedes-millions-of-workers-are-saying-i-quit
12. Salamon, S. D., & Robinson, S. L. (2008). Trust that binds: The impact of collective felt trust on organizational performance. *Journal of Applied Psychology, 93*(3), 593–601.
13. Meier, S., Stephenson, M., & Perkowski, P. (2019). Culture of trust and division of labor in nonhierarchical teams. *Strategic Management Journal, 40*(8), 1171–1193.
14. Brien, A. (1998). Professional ethics and the culture of trust. *Journal of Business Ethics, 17*(4), 391–409.
15. Mishra, A. K., Isaeva, N., Mishra, K. E., and Grubb, L. K. Top management teams and response to organizational crisis: The roles of trust, power, and control. Paper presented at the Journal of Management Studies Special Issue on Control and Trust Dynamics Paper Workshop (online), April 29–30.

14 HOW THE LEADER BUILDS A CULTURE OF TRUST

Change used to be welcomed only at the vending machine, and now, not even there!

–Aneil Kumar Howard Mishra

For Bob to institute such major cultural change in how people worked together and become engaged, it was critical that he and his leadership team had a common vision about how to best implement such a transformation. Having worked at several different General Motors (GM) locations, Bob knew how difficult it was to come out of a meeting in which everyone was really committed to decisions made during that meeting. Most decisions were driven from the top, lacking openness and transparency. He knew if his leadership team couldn't work together collaboratively, they couldn't eliminate all of the roadblocks they faced, and the change effort would likely fail.

His staff of very diverse and bright individuals all had different staff experiences at different GM locations in their careers. Neither Bob nor any of his staff had ever been in a working environment of complete trust. He and his team openly discussed the problem and collectively agreed they need the help of a consultant. Working with the consultant, they decided to have a two-day offsite over a weekend in an effort to establish the guidelines for developing truly mutual trust.

During the offsite, each member took a piece of paper and listed the strengths on one side and the weaknesses on the other for each member of the leadership team, including Bob. Then in a series of closed-door meetings, each staff member would review their perspective with one another. They were guided by the consultant not to argue, but rather only to ask questions to clarify their perceptions of one another. The goal was that if perception is indeed reality, then each person had better take a good look at themselves and try to understand what generated the other's perceptions. Most importantly, they also agreed to change their behavior based on those perceptions.

A great amount of time was spent on listening skills and creating a decision-making process that would ensure all voices were heard and respected on each item of every leadership team's agenda. They agreed to use the majority rule in which at least five of the nine team members had to agree. The critical difference in Bob's team's approach was that once a decision had been made, ALL members would give 100% effort to implement the decision, no matter how much any team member had fought for another option. In all the years that followed that working agreement, Bob said no one ever failed on the agreement.

The search and approach for building a trusting transparent relationship had been established. The above outline only provided a structure to internalize the process. Each member of the staff, including Bob, was responsible for an ongoing self-evaluation of their adherence to the agreement. In the beginning, they had meetings just to discuss their individual and collective performance. Those were very humbling discussions as each member would openly discuss where they could have done a better job.

Bob would be the first to tell us he was continually moving from one type of leadership role to another depending on the situation and the group of people he was dealing with. He often stated that maintaining his own self-esteem was critical to maximizing the potential of his workforce. He'd also be the first to admit that his ideas often fell short of those of his collective staff, the union leaders, or other respective workgroups. There were occasions, however, where his background and persuasiveness led to the best decision.

As time went on, Bob and his team began truly collaborating rather than simply implementing Bob's directives. From then on, anytime they saw a barrier to improving the culture, they knocked it down. They succeeded in this by changing the physical structure of the plant, including creating one central dining room in the middle of the plant for all employees: hourly, salaried, and upper management, eliminating the executive dining room in the process. In this way, Bob's team provided opportunities for the supervisors to communicate and get to know one another over meals and during break times. Of course, it also provided opportunities for hourly and salaried employees plant-wide to get to know one another in an environment separate from their regular work areas. As Bob says:

> Any time I went into the dining room, I'd go out of my way to talk to somebody whom I didn't know. I did this to encourage our salaried employees and managers to do the same with the hourly employees and with each other. This way, anybody could feel comfortable having lunch with a manager. To me, it was not a big deal. For them, they would go home and say to their spouses, "Guess who I had lunch with today? I had lunch with the plant manager."
>
> That really opened the culture up. Everyone would feel like "we're all here together. We're all people who have things to contribute to the organization." Then they started asking one another, "How do we work more effectively together and take advantage of each other's skills and capabilities?"

While efforts on improving relationships between supervisors and their hourly teams continued, Bob's team also began to work on strengthening relationships among the salaried supervisors because they did not like each other either: one group of supervisors did not like the machine repair supervisors and the machine repair supervisors did not like those who supervised the pipefitters.

Bob's team went further and abolished the rigid dress codes that separated hourly from salaried employees, and salaried employees from their managers—including the requirement that salaried employees wear a suit and tie. It is not surprising that the first time we met Bob, we were pleasantly surprised to find him wearing a sweater, which had become his basic uniform. It was a simple yet powerful way to let the hourly employees know that Bob was eliminating another division between them and the salaried employees.

Finally, Bob and his team eliminated separate parking lots for hourly and salaried employees and reserved parking spots for the top managers at the plant, including Bob's own parking spot.[1] As hourly employees typically arrived two hours before salaried employees, this meant that salaried employees now had a much longer walk to the plant, which was no fun during the Cleveland winters. If Bob arrived at the plant late, he would park at the back of the lot and walk all the way through it to get to the entrance to the building.

These moves were not just symbolic. The quality of the food on offer matters when people are working in stressful, often physically uncomfortable work environments, which were certainly more uncomfortable for those working on the factory floor than in the offices. Where someone is allowed to park also matters, especially during Cleveland's brutal winters.

Building your organizational culture has to be intentional. If the leader does not make a specific effort to create a positive, trustworthy culture, a negative, toxic one can form, especially under highly competitive business conditions. It takes effort and intention for a culture of trust to emerge. This is why leaders have such an important role. They cannot wait for someone else to set the standard for how people should treat one another in the organization. The organization's mission, vision, and values are where intentions are reinforced. Leaders can begin modeling what is expected within their own teams. It also follows that leaders need to remove those who act in ways that undermine the culture that is being built.

Culture is formed, then, as a natural progression of the specific leadership efforts initially taken by the leader and the top management team of an organization. When specific choices are made about how to treat employees or how to treat customers, culture is formed. Bob made intentional choices not only about who would stay on his leadership team, but about what kind of structure and policies he would preserve (or eliminate) in order to ensure a trustworthy culture. As president and cofounder of Rhino Foods, Ted Castle told us:

> Do you have a purpose, principles, and vision?? Do your practices and policies follow that or not? Our Employee Principle states that we establish mutual trust and respect with an environment for listening and personal expression. Trust is something that can be broken quickly and takes so long to build, so you must keep asking these questions.

Aneil's college friend Hal Stern shared how he builds culture:

> When joining an organization as its leader, I aggressively listen
> and learn the language of the organization and its stakeholders. If
> you don't find the clues about change, tension, and driving the cul-
> tural attributes you want, then you've immediately impaired that
> "derivative of idea movement."

In his 1994 book *Leadership and the Culture of Trust*, the late Virginia
Commonwealth University professor Gilbert Fairholm described the way
leadership and trust intersect in this way: "Leadership takes place in a context
of mutual trust based on shared vision, ideals and values."[2] It is the leader's
job, then, to build this mutual trust by sharing their vision, ideals, and values,
all while working with their employees to ensure that they are all in agreement about them.

What follows in this chapter are a number of critical ways in which leaders can foster a culture of trust. It is not realistic to assume that they must be
adopted in any particular order, or that all of them are equally influential.
Since organizational cultures are both unique and have comparable attributes,
some of these methods may be relatively more important in some organizations, but each of them is expected to have a significant role in enhancing the
ROCC of Trust throughout the organization.

CREATING AN OPEN-DOOR POLICY

One way that Bob was able to quickly build trusting relationships with his
10,000 employees was by instituting an open-door policy. This meant that he
was available anytime any employee (union or salaried) wanted to talk to him
about anything. This might be intimidating to an employee who was several
levels removed from reporting to Bob, but he wanted to remove any barriers
between him and his employees. He really wanted to get the message across
that he was accessible.

We had the opportunity to see Bob's open-door policy in action during
a visit to Parma almost 30 years ago. We were there to interview Bob and 30
members of his team for a case study we were writing about him and the
Parma plant. As we waited in Bob's office for the interview, he asked us to
leave. One of his employees had knocked on the door and he needed to speak
with him—immediately. Bob kept his word and made himself available, as
promised. Because he kept this promise, employees continued to feel comfortable coming to him, sharing their problems, ideas, and solutions.

Due to the nature of a leader's position—and with it their power and
visibility among other factors—we believe that a leader setting an example
from the top of an organization is critical in motivating people to develop
the ROCC of Trust with others. To be intentional about building trust
as a new leader, you will have to "be like Bob" and walk the talk. When
Bob asked us to leave his office to uphold his open-door policy, he was

demonstrating that he could be trusted (both by us and, more importantly, by his employees). He was a) doing what he said he would do (be reliable); b) be accessible (be open for a conversation); c) show his competence (by helping to solve a problem); and d) show his concern for his employees (by putting them first). It is not enough to say that you can be trusted; you must show others that they can trust you by your actions. When Bob followed through on his promise to have an open door, this encouraged his employees to take on more ownership in the business—in other words, to become more engaged.

BUILDING A TRUST-BASED TEAM AT THE TOP

Building trusted leadership is an especially useful way to begin building a culture of trust. For example, supporting a culture of shared leadership within teams, with its norms of egalitarianism and mutual accountability, is consistent with developing a culture of trust.[3] Another is having shared goals. Human resources executive Steve Fitzgerald explained the role of shared goals as he builds a team:

> When filling senior roles, I make sure that they understand that what we do is based on shared goals. If you and I agree that the goal is what matters, then our choices and decisions should be in pursuit of achieving that shared goal. I trust people who make those choices rather than ones that are self-beneficial or self-aggrandizing. One of the reasons why we're not (still) wandering around in loincloths is because we're able to collaborate around shared goals. I find people who aren't willing to subordinate themselves and their own interests at times to those goals to be untrustworthy.

Even if someone is not the top leader per se, intentionally building trust with fellow top management team members, as well as with one's subordinates, contributes toward building a culture of trust. Our former GM mentor Anita Johnson indicated how building those interpersonal relationships among the team contributes to team trust:

> As an HR/LR [labor relations] leader I have always set up meetings with key functional leaders in the organization to introduce myself, and to identify key successes and challenges they have had and/or are facing and connect with them on a personal level if possible. This helps build the interpersonal relationships, and provides knowledge to start the process of prioritizing key actions that my team and I can take to provide value to the organization and become a strategic business partner.

I also spend time individually with my team members to get to know them, identify initial strengths and developmental opportunities, and what they value. Recognizing these team members is also important, and what is required to move the organization to the next level. These steps help build trust, foster communication, and promote excellence in the work to be performed.

ESTABLISH THE RIGHT VISION AND MISSION

Mike Gannon shared that starting with the right vision or mission is essential in building a culture of trust:

> A key strategy for establishing a trust-based culture is to establish a clear and compelling vision of what we ultimately want to achieve as an organization. Not only does it explain where the organization is heading, it also provides an opportunity for people to feel part of something larger than themselves.
>
> My vision for the HR function was to make the company successful. If we did everything we wanted to as a function and the company was not successful, obviously we had not worked on the right things. The biggest change was establishing a formal HR purpose statement focused on attracting and retaining great people, developing people's strengths and putting them in the right jobs, and creating an environment where everyone had the opportunity to contribute and excel. This was ultimately shortened to: "Right People! Right Job! Right Environment!" In due course, the HR purpose statement was imprinted into the minds of the global HR team, as well as many others in the broader organization.

In discussing his own efforts to build a culture of trust, Jeremy Kane, the head of a Michigan marketing consulting firm, stated:

> In building our organization's culture, we needed a clear, shared vision; management decisions aligned and consistent with that vision. We also needed a clear definition of expectations and rewards for each person on the team. We identified the company's new leaders and provided them challenges and learning experiences. We instituted decisive mentoring and management of team performance, and frequent and clear reporting of progress. Trust came partly from this shared vision as well as from a compatibility in values. This trust then galvanized effort toward shared goals so that successes and challenges were shared.
>
> When trust is formed, it also energizes my efforts because I feel a sense not only of personal achievement, but also a contribution to the shared goals and successes of the company and my team.

ENGAGING EACH EMPLOYEE

Engaged employees are committed to the organization's goals, know how to contribute to its mission, and want to do their best work, leading to better organizational performance.[4] When a leader has built a culture of trust, this catalyzes employee engagement.[5] As Mike Gannon told us:

> Many organizations develop visions and purpose statements, but they are worthless if people do not understand what is intended, if leaders do not live it, and if it does not become part of the fabric of how work is done. My personal goal was that every HR team member would instinctively and confidently know what "Mike" would want to have done without having to ask anyone about it.
>
> I have found that employees need three important ingredients to successfully navigate the change process: *empathy*, someone who will listen, be nonjudgmental; *information*, an intellectual understanding of "why"; and *hope*, through ideas, options, plans, and possibilities for the future. When I failed to lead change once, it was because we had checked the boxes on information and hope but had totally neglected empathy. We also had no reservoir of trust to rely upon.
>
> To successfully lead organizational change, I believe a leader must acknowledge that change is painful and that their people need empathy and compassion. It is also important to name the feelings people are experiencing and sincerely listen and understand that *everyone* has to go through the following steps when undertaking organizational change: shock and denial, anger and depression, then acceptance and integration.
>
> It is not healthy to skip any of the steps nor to get stuck on any one step for long. For example, when people express anger about a change, it is a normal and necessary part of the process. The time to worry is when the anger is bottled up inside and not getting out. The key is to help your people move quickly and steadily through each phase of the process, and the best way to accomplish that is to establish a foundation of trust.

Engaging employees also involves regularly taking the pulse of employees, as Anita Johnson did. She advises:

> Change is often adopted more easily if there is engagement from those impacted by the change. Spend time determining a specific communication plan with a "no surprises" approach for impacted persons. Following communication and implementation, it is important to conduct periodic check-ins and assessments to determine whether the change has met expectations and/or if additional

adjustments are needed. Sometimes there are those individuals who are not quickly accepting of the change and additional support and/or reinforcement are needed.

In our own research on employee engagement, we have found that there are several ways that leaders can improve engagement and employees' trust in their organization.[6] One way, confirmed by research undertaken by Gallup, is by helping employees understand and use their strengths at work.[7] When employees are able to use the gifts and talents that they have, they are more excited and motivated to help the organization achieve its goals.

Our own research has further found that employees are also more engaged when they receive regular feedback from their supervisors.[8] Rather than wait for an annual review, employees are more engaged when they get frequent feedback about their job from their boss, similar to how a coach would provide encouragement to improve performance. Employees also appreciate receiving praise from their employer, as well as opportunities to grow in their job. Ultimately, the best bosses show employees that they care about them and their careers as much as they care about their own.

Not engaging employees, in contrast, is a surefire way to fail in building a culture of trust and can foster significant resistance to any cultural change effort. Mike Gannon experienced this himself. He recounts:

> The biggest disaster of my career was the result of some of the best work I have ever done. When I worked at GM in the late 1980s, a new executive vice president (EVP) was hired to lead a major culture change in the company. (He was the first of a long line of people hired to achieve the same goal.) He wanted to institute a strict forced-ranking system to evaluate employee performance, and he picked me to develop and implement the process.
>
> I was in my early thirties and thrilled to lead such an important project. I was able to recruit a great team of very talented people to help me get the job done. We studied what other companies were doing, developed detailed policies and procedures, created brochures and training materials, and even did some videos (not used very often in those days) to illustrate how to deliver difficult messages to employees. From a technical perspective, it was a near-perfect job. From a human-dynamics perspective, however, it was a catastrophe.
>
> We knew there would be some pushback, but we all assumed (and I think the EVP did as well) that because the EVP approved the plan, and the CEO had agreed to it, the new policies would simply be implemented, and no other actions would be required. We could not have been more wrong.
>
> On purpose, we had not involved the HR community very much in the development process because the EVP did not want his new

policy to be smothered by the "old culture." As a result, we had little support or commitment from the HR function who would be implementing the policy. The EVP had also not done very much to build true buy-in from the executive leadership team for his culture-change ideas, and we had done nothing to really prepare the workforce—and their supervisors—for such consequential change. Worst of all, there was no reservoir of trust to draw upon to help make the change happen. In fact, we had created a negative balance of trust.

As a result, the policy changes lasted about two weeks before the backlash from employees, supervisors, the HR community, and senior management was so strong that the new policies were abruptly canceled. Shortly thereafter, the new EVP left the company, and I was left wondering how to pick up the tattered pieces of my career.

Building a culture of trust takes effort and intention. It also takes reflection: Am I on the right track? Is this what is best for my organization? What are the implications/results of my actions (or inactions) as I build this culture of trust?

Questions to Consider

- What you would say is your organization's vision or mission, and is it widely understood AND accepted?
- Do the top executives of your organization demonstrate that they trust one another? Why, or why not?
- What are your organization's key practices for fostering employee engagement?

Notes

1. This only changed later after he had undergone some surgery and the employees all insisted that he take a parking spot next to the plant entrance. In our mind, that said a lot about the respect the union and employees had for Bob, in that they cared about his well-being and insisted that he take a spot of honor during his recovery.
2. Fairholm, G. W. (1994). *Leadership and the culture of trust*. Greenwood Publishing Group.
3. Brien, A. (1998). Professional ethics and the culture of trust. *Journal of Business Ethics*, 17(4), 391–409.
4. Royal, K. (2019). What engaged employees do differently. Gallup Workplace, 1–11.
5. Ilyas, S., Abid, G., & Ashfaq, F. (2020). Ethical leadership in sustainable organizations: The moderating role of general self-efficacy and the mediating role of organizational trust. *Sustainable Production and Consumption*, 22, 195–204.

6. Mishra, K. E., Boynton, L., & Mishra, A. K. (2014). Driving employee engagement: The expanded role of internal communications, *International Journal of Business Communication, 51*(2/April), 183–202.

7. Harter, J. (2020, February 4). *4 Factors Driving Record-High Employee Engagement in U.S.* Gallup. https://www.gallup.com/workplace/284180/factors-driving-record-high-employee-engagement.aspx

8. Mishra, Karen E., Boynton, Lois & Mishra, Aneil K. (2014). Driving employee engagement: The expanded role of internal communications, *International Journal of Business Communication, 51* (2), 183–202.

15

CEMENTING **A** CULTURE **OF** TRUST

Several years before GM announced with great fanfare that it was instituting "diagonal slice meetings" in the mid-1980s, in which top managers of a division or group would have coffee or lunch with a cross-section of employees from different areas and levels in the hierarchy, Bob had already begun holding his own such meetings:

> I had all kinds of "slices." I had meetings with teams, one-on-one meetings, groups of teams, diagonal slices, all kinds of ways we brought people together. Of course, the diagonal slice is a really good one, where you get different people at different levels and different parts of the organization to come in and talk about how they looked at the business.

The diagonal slices, in particular, were very difficult to work through. Many participants did not know one another, so they first started off by giving their name and key responsibilities. Then, Bob would ask them how they perceived the business plan was being implemented and how they viewed their jobs. Many of them were very reluctant to talk:

> This is because they grew up in a culture where if they said something that pissed somebody off, that person would then kick their ass after work. Not everybody could handle being that open. If I went in there and people weren't talking, and then I acted in any way that might be considered demeaning or threatening, boy, they just shut down.

> I had to learn how to build chemistry quickly and to hold engaging conversations in settings like that. If a couple of people responded to something I said, then I would get them to open up a bit: "Hey, George, in the area where you work, what's your thought on this?" Even though they did not traditionally interact with upper-level managers, they learned how to do it.

> As time went on, and people realized that nobody was going to lose their job by being open, the conversations deepened. They would then go back to their respective work groups and say "Gee, I just sat down with a manager and one of the superintendents."

DOI: 10.4324/9780367822170-19

MAINTAINING FOCUS

Leaders and their organizations will inevitably face both internal and external forces or events that can inhibit efforts to build and maintain a culture of trust. These can include internal events, such as new leadership, and external forces, such as a pandemic, economic downturn, or sharpened competition. All of these can interrupt the trust that has been built if you are not aware of how they might impact on your culture.

The challenge, then, is to leverage established trust to combat those forces. If you allow external forces to prevent you from maintaining your reliability, you lose the trust others have in you. If you allow them to undermine your transparency and openness, trust is diminished. If you allow them to interfere with the way you do business, causing others to question your capability or competency, your trustworthiness is harmed. Finally, if you allow them to prevent you from showing your stakeholders that you sincerely care about them and their best interests, you have affected your ability to be seen as a trustworthy organization and/or culture. This is again why leadership is intentional: Leaders need to be aware of how changes to their organization can impact the trust they have built and fight hard to prevent it from interrupting the culture of trust.

Our former GM boss Mike Gannon shared how he knew that the organizational culture was on the right track:

> One of the goals I set for the global HR team was to win "great place to work" awards in three locations within three years. Thanks to lots of hard work, dedication, and the fruits of a trust-based organization, we received recognition in three different locations around the globe. While the awards themselves were not important, they provided some tangible, outside confirmation that we were on the right track, and reinforced the commitment to our trust-based culture.

REINFORCING CULTURE THROUGH PRACTICES, SYSTEMS, AND PROCESSES

To maintain a culture of trust, that culture's beliefs, norms, values, and behaviors cannot depend solely on the leader or even a group of individuals for reinforcement. Rather, the formal organization must also reinforce the informal elements—in other words, the culture. Formal elements include training and development, performance management, and reward systems, as well as written practices, processes, and rules that remind people what constitutes trustworthy behavior. Mike Gannon shared how he was able to cement his team's culture:

> A good way to encourage and "cement" a culture is to find people and teams doing what your vision calls for and elevate and recognize their contributions. One of our goals was to be a "world class" HR function. To help

make that a reality, we established and awarded World-Class HR awards annually.

Individuals and teams could self-nominate for achievements that were world class in the categories of a) new HR process or system, b) one-time response to a major HR issue, c) extraordinary professional achievement, or d) "shamelessly stealing" a world-class idea from another company location or from an outside organization. The winners (usually about 15 awards) came from all levels of the HR team and from all our regions.

We presented the awards in an Academy Award-type ceremony with suitable trophies, and I wore a tux as the master of ceremonies. Most importantly, a story accompanied each award to explain what was being recognized and why it was world class. The awards were lots of fun, highly sought after, and helped to make real the level of performance we were seeking. People also started believing that we were not that far from being world class.

NAVIGATING NECESSARY CHANGES

Inevitably, leaders will need to make a strategic change, either to pursue significant new opportunities or to respond to changing external conditions. When that happens, how they manage this will either enhance or diminish the trust that has been established. Mike Gannon noted the role of trust when instituting such changes:

> When a significant change is announced, the first question people ask themselves is: "What does this mean for me?"
>
> I find a trap leaders fall into, especially in technical functions, is thinking or hoping that people are like programmable machines that will quickly adapt to change if it is explained logically. I agree that the rationale must be logical, but unfortunately logic is not a big part of how humans deal with change. Because of our nature, a large part of the change process is emotional, and leaders must acknowledge this fact in order to be successful.
>
> The change process is emotional because change always comes with loss, and loss always comes with fear and pain. We always seek to avoid fear and pain and stay in our comfort zone, even if it is not a great place. But with change also comes opportunity, opportunity that we will miss if we don't get out of our comfort zone.
>
> So how do you get people to move out of their comfort zone and risk fear and pain for the chance of new opportunity? The answer is trust. People need to trust that those leading the change process have the best interests of their people and the organization in mind.

Questions to Consider

- How can you stay aware of the external and internal events that might interrupt the trust you have built in your culture?
- How can you encourage change without damaging trust?
- How can you plan for the future while keeping your culture of trust in place?
- Now, we will explore each part of the ROCC in detail as it relates to building a culture of trust.

16
BUILDING **A CULTURE OF** RELIABILITY

The Parma plant's cultural change began to get noticed by GM's top corporate executives, and some of them, an executive vice president and his lieutenants, decided to visit the plant to see these changes for themselves. The day before their visit, they changed their schedule and instead of arriving early in the morning as planned, they were to come during lunch time. This would mean that the majority of employees would be eating rather than working at their stations. Bob really wanted the executives to see the plant in action because "we were doing so many wonderful things." He then decided to move up lunch to an earlier time. He had hundreds of notices printed and distributed throughout the plant, saying, "We'll be changing the lunch hours …" He recalls:

> I thought everybody understood. We have an opportunity to show exactly what we're doing. We don't want to do anything half-assed just for some lunch. That's the way I saw it.
>
> Then, Roger Montgomery, the head of Shop Committee, which was responsible for reviewing all the plant's operations from the local UAW's standpoint, came in holding one of the notices, and said, "Bob, you got to be kidding me." I asked, "What do you mean?" He replied, "You really mean this?" I said, "Yes, I mean it. You understand why I want to do it." Roger replied, "Yes, I understand, but you've got thousands of other people who won't understand why they have to change their lunch hour for three or four people visiting the plant. They'll never buy it."
>
> He was right of course. I called the executive vice president's secretary and asked, "Is there any way their arrival time could be changed?" and she said, "No problem," and switched their arrival with another visit they had that day, so the executives could arrive before our lunch break. As a result, they were able to see the significant positive changes that were taking place, and that provided us with important additional support from the top brass.
>
> To me, it was so easy. "Who gives a crap about lunch when you're talking about the future of our plant?" I initially had the position of, "Screw it. We're going to do it this way because I want these

DOI: 10.4324/9780367822170-20

guys to see everything. The changed lunch hours stand." But, with how I was trying to change the organization, that certainly wasn't appropriate. I had to really listen to gain a different perspective.

Reliability is the first way we can show that we are trusted. Likewise, creating a reliable organization might just be the first way your employees or customers will know to trust you. At the organizational level, reliability is built through practices, systems, and metrics. A culture of reliability shows that your product was delivered as promised. A culture of reliability illustrates that your service will be on time, as expected. Sometimes, our organization may not even have the chance to show our competence if we are not reliable first. If we do not show up or arrive as scheduled, our customers will never know if we can be trusted to deliver as promised. Many organizations make big promises but never deliver. This is the first and simplest way to show others that your organization can be trusted: show up, arrive on time, answer the phone, and respond to the email in a timely fashion.

In their book on the subject of competing values, our Michigan mentors describe the role of metrics for demonstrating reliability: "Value creation is judged by well-defined metrics using short time horizons."[1] Aneil's mentor Dan Denison and his colleagues have also shown that firms with cultures that focus on consistency are more profitable.[2]

THE POWER OF SMALL WINS

Building on the work of Frederick Herzberg, organizational psychologists, Teresa Amabile and Steven Kramer, remind us that employees are motivated by the feeling of progress, which can be reinforced by a strategy of focusing on small wins.[3] Our GM mentor, Mike Gannon, developed a culture of reliability through a series of small actions that combined to have a large effect:

> I have found that listening to others always produces some hot-button ideas that are relatively easy to implement. Quickly implement as many of these initiatives as fit your overall strategy, and give credit based on the feedback that resulted in these changes. For example:

- HR leaders told us they wanted more collaboration among them, so we started having weekly staff meetings by the following month.
- Employees said they wanted more information about what was happening in the company, so we started quarterly functional meetings the following month.
- The senior leadership of the company said they wanted more input into filling key openings, so we established a monthly human capital committee that met with the CEO's direct reports.

Implementing the quick wins and giving credit and value to the feedback I received helped establish that I was a reliable and open leader.

Aneil's colleague Steve Fitzgerald shares how **Reliability** and **Openness** go hand in hand as he looks to hire new people:

> In looking to hire people in senior roles, I talk to their references to explore whether they do what they say they're going to do, because that's what trust is rooted in. It's just that simple. I really don't care about how they handled a particular problem. When someone says to me that they're going to do something and then they don't do it, I have trouble continuing to interact with that person because I hold myself to a really high standard.

Demonstrating reliability, then, is the first way you can show that you can be trusted. Next, we will consider how to build openness and transparency within your organization, the second part of the ROCC of Trust.

Questions to Consider

- Do you agree that you can demonstrate reliability first? What can you begin doing to show others that you are reliable?
- What company can you benchmark that is excellent at demonstrating reliability? What can you learn from them that you can use now?
- What is a small win that you can create right now?

Notes

1. Cameron, K. S., Quinn, R. E., DeGraff, J., & Thakor, A. V. (2014). *Competing values leadership* (p. 90). Edward Elgar Publishing.
2. Kotrba, L. M., Gillespie, M. A., Schmidt, A. M., Smerek, R. E., Ritchie, S. A., & Denison, D. R. (2012). Do consistent corporate cultures have better business performance? Exploring the interaction effects. *Human Relations, 65*(2), 241–262.
3. Amabile, T. M., & Kramer, S. J. (2011). The power of small wins. *Harvard Business Review, 89*(5), 70–80.

17 BUILDING A CULTURE OF OPENNESS

When Bob Lintz was the new leader at GM Parma, he knew that it would be important for his team to trust each other before they could collectively build trust with the rest of the plant's staff. In describing his approach to building trust with his top management team, Bob emphasized the essential importance of first addressing the interpersonal aspects of working together, such as working together as a team, and of making decisions for the good of the plant:

> Getting my team involved and committed to the vision meant asking them to open up about their inner feelings and to voice any frustrations they had. They wanted to know how I really felt about them, and I wanted to learn how they felt about each other. They wanted to know where they stood, and where their careers were headed. We talked about any politics being played in the organization. Most of that is pretty well-guarded information, for fear of consequences from speaking up.

> It was my role to get people to open up. I understood the consequences, and I also knew how difficult it was to open up. I was able to get my immediate staff to agree to go out after work, on our own time, and really talk about these issues. We needed to develop a relationship of openness where we could really, really say how we felt without threat of reprisal. That took some time, but once that was established, then trust with one another just mushroomed.

If **Reliability** is about processes and measurement, **Openness** is about communicating those processes widely and sharing results transparently. Measure what is important and disseminate widely. Jenny Meyer, president and CEO of a Houston, Texas energy industry consulting firm, described the importance of practicing transparency with her clients:

> Integrity is very important to us; transparency with our clients is very important to us. I'm the weird third-party vendor that shares my own budget spreadsheet with clients.

DOI: 10.4324/9780367822170-21

TRANSPARENCY AND OPENNESS

Kim Cameron and his colleagues found that firms with open cultures are able to share knowledge and are more innovative. Leaders in such cultures are humble enough to know when they do not have all the answers and are open to new ideas in order to grow.[1] This is much easier to do when things are going well, but harder when there are external challenges to the organization.[2]

Our own research has found that when top management teams promote openness in their companies, their employees trust both the top management team and one another to a greater degree. This approach to internal communications is a form of internal marketing, which lets employees know that they are a priority to the organization and on a par with other stakeholders, such as customers, suppliers, and the surrounding community.[3]

The best form of internal communication is two-way communication, in which employees have an opportunity not only to receive feedback from their bosses, but also to have the opportunity to give feedback to them in return. When management truly listens to what employees are saying, this builds trust by letting employees know that their feedback is valued.[4] Most recently, employees have cited this lack of listening to them as one reason for the "Great Resignation." One study found that four out of five employees do not feel heard.[5] When employees do not feel heard or valued, they will take their talents and skills elsewhere.

A LISTENING TOUR

Mike Gannon described how he used openness and transparency in a new role, which allowed him to build trust:

> In 2013, I began a new job as the CHRO for a global manufacturing company with headquarters in Hong Kong, facilities in more than 20 global locations, and substantial manufacturing and engineering capacity located in the People's Republic of China. When my predecessor retired, he left me with the foundation for a strong HR function, but the function clearly needed to "raise its game" to help the company succeed in a very competitive environment. Most importantly, there were morale and trust issues within both the HR team and other pockets of the company.
>
> I spent most of the first 90 days on the job conducting a listening tour. I visited many locations around the globe to understand what people thought about the HR team, what HR needed to improve, and what our priorities should be. Besides the CEO and the senior management team, I spent time with as many members of the global HR team as I could, as well as key internal customers of HR services. Toward the end of that process, I would start to share with people some of my preliminary conclusions and ask them to validate them.

Demonstrating that you are open to new ideas, providing and receiving feedback, and being willing to share information are all ways you can build a culture of openness. Next, we will consider how to build competence within your organization.

Questions to Consider

- What are the primary ways in which top management communicates with the rest of your organization?
- Who are your important stakeholders, and what do they need to hear about from you regularly?
- What can you do to promote two-way communication with your employees?

Notes

1. Cameron, K. S., Quinn, R. E., DeGraff, J., & Thakor, A. V. (2014). *Competing values leadership*. Edward Elgar Publishing.
2. Cameron, K. (2012). *Positive leadership: Strategies for extraordinary performance*. Berrett-Koehler Publishers.
3. Mishra, K., Boynton, L., & Mishra, A. (2014). Driving employee engagement: The expanded role of internal communications. *International Journal of Business Communication, 51*(2), 183–202.
4. Mishra, K., Boynton, L., & Mishra, A. (2014). Driving employee engagement: The expanded role of internal communications. *International Journal of Business Communication, 51*(2), 183–202.
5. Douglas, E. (2021, Kune3). *Four in five employees don't feel heard – here's why*. Human Resources Director. https://www.hcamag.com/ca/specialization/hr-technology/four-in-five-employees-dont-feel-heard-heres-why/259493

18

BUILDING **A** CULTURE **OF** COMPETENCE

In the mid-1980s, as part of implementing the team concept at Parma, a transformative way in which the UAW and its hourly employees worked together with salaried employees and management, Bob invested in tens of thousands of hours and $25 million on training on interpersonal and group dynamics, problem-solving in teams, and effective communication. The training involved groups of roughly 20 different hourly and salaried employees each, representing different operations within the plant. The first 40-hour week of training was spent on interpersonal dynamics, including self-evaluations, as well as identifying individual, group, and organizational responsibilities. The second week focused on team building and problem solving. Finally, the emphasis during the third week was on how to communicate effectively, both in teams and sets of teams.

Concurrent with all this training, Bob and his management team were able to negotiate a radical reclassification of eight unskilled job classes into one basic classification, which resulted in much greater flexibility on the work floor. Now, operators would be responsible for their own work areas, including basic maintenance, rather than having to wait for specially classified workers, including sweepers or janitors, to do the work.

The other important work role innovation was the creation of a new Team Coordinator role—this was an hourly employee, typically elected by their peers. This person's primary job was to set the agenda for and run all team meetings, responsibilities that were previously part of the salaried supervisor's job. This supervisor still attended team meetings and formally signed off on decisions made by the team, but the team essentially became self-governing. Four union employees received specialized training to be Team Counselors; their job was to help supervisors who had identified a need for additional skill development or coaching on how to run team meetings for their team coordinators. These innovations did not take place at other GM operations until many years later, if at all.

Jay Barney and colleagues have found that employees who invest in themselves contribute to their firms' competitive advantage.[1] In addition, although the skills that employees learn might often be tied to their particular job or company, self-investment signals to other firms that these employees are dedicated enough to invest in themselves generally, making them attractive recruitment targets.

DOI: 10.4324/9780367822170-22

Managed correctly, human capital enhances organizational performance because employees, after all, are the ones who implement a firm's strategy.[2] Indeed, Dave Ulrich and his colleagues have found in their research that building a culture that focuses on talent can help an organization outperform their competitors.[3]

BUILD A CULTURE OF STRENGTHS

One of our favorite tools for assessing and enhancing human capital is Gallup's Clifton Strengths.[4] We have found this to be a particularly powerful way for individuals to identify their own strengths (and weaknesses) and to see how collaborating with others in teams allows them to complement those strengths and offset these weaknesses, thereby contributing to a culture of competence. The StrengthsFinder assessment can be used in many different ways and at various times: as part of onboarding or initial training, when assigning jobs, or in talent development or success planning.

By understanding employee strengths, you ensure that employees are in the right job that will help them succeed, based on what they can do best. A recent Axios article indicates that 16% of new graduates want upskilling from their employers.[5] This demonstrates that even after college students graduate, they continue to want to learn and grow to build upon their strengths.

Competence makes any change effort more sustainable. Jeremy Kane explained how achieving company goals depends on two things: improving employee performance and not allowing the benefits of interpersonal relationships among team members to become more important than the needs of the business:

> We failed as leaders when we didn't develop people to their fullest potential. By failing to address shortcomings of team members rather than compensating for them, and by not providing enough constructive criticism and mentorship to help talented employees, our company performance suffering.
>
> I could also have been more flexible in my expectations by accepting that there might be several ways to accomplish the same goal. As a result, I have learned to separate the company needs from my own and evaluate situations and people with the company needs in mind. This limits the influence of my interpersonal relationships with team members over the key decisions to be made.

THE COERCIVE POWER FALLACY

Mike Gannon shared how leaders can empower employees to build a culture of competence:

> In my experience, many leaders overestimate the effectiveness of coercive power. Yes, powerful leaders can order things done. But

if the result is half-hearted compliance, foot-dragging, subtle sabotage, and a fearful and demoralized workforce, will lasting change really be accomplished? Of course, a leader can invest enormous resources to constantly follow up and punish or reward individuals for their compliance. But in my experience, except in the face of an existential threat to the organization, the opportunity cost of using coercive power to initiate change is rarely justified.

A few years ago, one of my key subordinates was very frustrated with me about how I wanted to implement a new company-wide HR policy. I told her that I wanted to start with a pilot program in parts of the organization that wanted the new policy and had prepared their teams for the change. Once success had been demonstrated (and we could address any flaws), more leaders would want the policy for their team, and soon after that, we could roll out the policy to the entire company.

My subordinate said that I was the SVP [senior vice president] of HR and should just order it done. I agreed I could do just that, but reminded her that our product was not a PowerPoint presentation but rather a successful policy change that would improve the performance of the company. I told her that while I had the power to order it done, I did not have the resources to force it to be successfully implemented.

I chose to promote from within people who were already exhibiting the desired behaviors and who were well-respected. By doing so, I was not only able to quickly have leaders fully committed to the new direction, but also signal to other talented people that they could have a future with the company. Finally, I carefully added very strong talent from the outside to help drive change, provide new insights, and to complement my own strengths. I believe it is important to show that you want people on your team that could one day replace you.

While separating people is never pleasant, it is sometimes required. I believe that almost all people who reach leadership positions are competent, but as organizational needs change, their skillset and strengths may no longer fit their current organization. I did replace some HR leaders because they were no longer a good fit for what we were trying to accomplish. The process was done with as much care and respect as possible, and most found good positions in other companies.

I also believe that although people may be relieved when you remove a "problematic" leader, nobody wants that leader to be treated poorly. Not only is the leader owed respect but failing to treat them well causes others in the organization to worry about how you might treat them.

Next, we will focus on creating a culture of caring, an overlooked aspect of leadership.

Questions to Consider

- How much in the way of tangible resources does your organization devote toward training employees?
- Who does the training in your organization? Can they help employees understand their strengths and improve their career satisfaction?
- Is the training focused on real work or is it separated from it?

Notes

1. Morris, S. S., Alvarez, S. A., Barney, J. B., & Molloy, J. C. (2017). Firm-specific human capital investments as a signal of general value: Revisiting assumptions about human capital and how it is managed. *Strategic Management Journal, 38*(4), 912–919.
2. Becker, B. E., Huselid, M. A., & Ulrich, D. (2002). Six key principles for measuring human capital performance in your organization. *Business and Society Review, 1*, 71–75.
3. Ulrich, D., & Brockbank, W. (2016). Creating a winning culture: Next step for leading HR professionals. *Strategic HR Review, 15*(2), 51–56.
4. For further information, please visit https://www.gallup.com/cliftonstrengths/en/252137/home.aspx
5. Pandey, E. (2021, September 14). *What young people want from their employers*. Axios. https://www.axios.com/young-workers-employer-social-issues-poll-17926385-8c63-4786-838d-4f040472164f.html

19

BUILDING **A** CULTURE OF CARING

As another way to build a culture of trust based on caring, Bob and his team created "new business" teams composed of both hourly/union employees and salaried employees or managers to make presentations in front of GM executives and representatives of the UAW in Detroit to win new business for the Parma plant. At first, their pitches were regularly rejected. In and of themselves, these joint pitches contributed to eliminating some distrust between hourly and salaried employees, because historically the local UAW believed that Parma's management was deliberately failing to get new business, as a way to gain concessions from the union. However, when hourly employees came back to Parma from their presentations made at GM headquarters, reporting that both GM executives *and* top UAW officials had given them feedback that their proposals were not competitive enough, then the local union realized that Bob and his managers were telling the truth that the plant had to transform how work got done.

These joint pitches also created a sense of shared fate between the union and management, between hourly and salaried employees. As Parma began to win new business and that success resulted in greater job security for everyone, the culture of caring was strengthened. Indeed, as Parma continued to not only survive but thrive, by 1998 the local union voluntarily gave up $20 million in contractual overtime pay because they believed that the money would be better spent on further modernization of the facility. This meant the average union employee gave up $10,000 in overtime pay, with some employees in the skilled trades relinquishing $25,000—which is about $17,000 and $43,000, respectively, in 2021 value.

We are often asked if it is possible to teach others to create a culture of caring. Jane Dutton and colleagues, in their research on compassion at work, note that such a culture is built through cooperation.[1] When the organization creates renewable resources, such as trust, connections, and positive emotions, it will strengthen shared values and beliefs, such as dignity and respect, which in turn cultivates other relational skills and the willingness to collaborate.[2] Professors Emma Seppälä and Kim Cameron found that positive cultures embrace compassion as a lubricant to help those who are struggling.[3] In fact, positive leaders who offer compassion are able to build a resilient workforce, especially in times of crisis.

Even as Rhino Foods has grown to more than $60 million in annual revenue, Ted Castle and his company have found a way to build a culture of caring in a variety of ways. In 2007, in partnership with the United Way of Chittenden

DOI: 10.4324/9780367822170-23

County, Vermont it began its Working Bridges Program. Working Bridges is a collaborative effort by progressive employers in Chittenden County to facilitate the development and implementation of innovative workplace practices to improve employee productivity, retention, advancement, and financial stability. In the past decade and a half since then, Rhino Foods has assumed a leadership role in this collaboration—piloting several workplace practices under the Working Bridges concept that have been extremely successful. Rhino Foods credits its Working Bridges Program with reducing employee turnover from 40% to only 15%, and with helping improve the financial well-being and stability of its frontline employees. Several new programs have been created and implemented as a result of the project, including Income Advance Loan program, Financial Literacy training, an onsite Resource Coordinator, and Bridges Out of Poverty™ training for supervisors.

The company also credits its Employee Exchange program with "saving thousands of dollars in staffing costs while retaining their skilled employees in the long term."[4] This program hires out employees to other businesses rather than laying them off in slack periods, which began in 1993.[5] In partnership with North Country Federal Credit Union, an Income Advance Loan program was also developed and implemented by Rhino Foods, resulting in over $350,000 in short-term no questions asked or credit score required loans to employees, which have addressed various needs. Employees repay the loans through a payroll deduction. Once the loan is repaid, they don't turn off the deduction (unless the employee asks) and the deduction flows to a savings account. The program has helped many employees remain employed, transition from financial crisis to savings, and truly get on the path to building solid credit and improving their financial stability.[6]

SHARE CREDIT

Mike Gannon shared his lesson of the "Glory Berry Bush," a philosophy that builds a culture of caring and compassion by sharing credit with others on your team.

> During a college internship, I had a boss explain to me his ideas about the proper care and feeding of an organization. In his mind, all organizations had a "glory berry" bush. The purpose of the glory berry bush was to recognize and reward individuals and teams for doing good things. The reward was getting to pick some of the berries. The unfortunate thing about the glory berry bush, however, was that the berries were limited, and new berries grew only very slowly.

> My boss said that some people were so greedy that, when given a chance to visit the glory berry bush, they picked all the berries off for themselves and left none for anyone else. As a result, these people were despised by their colleagues. Others, he said, were too shy to pick the berries, and were also disliked by their co-workers. He said the trick was to pick just the right number of berries when asked to visit the glory berry bush.

His advice to me when I became a leader was to be last in line for the glory. Let your people go first, and then be generous and invite others in the organization that helped accomplish your goal to also pick some berries. He added, of course, that when it was my turn, there might not be many berries left, but that I should still always leave some behind. He explained that if I followed his advice, I would eventually have more glory berries than anyone else in the organization. Why? Because I would always have a winning team making many trips to the glory berry bush, and as a result there would always be a great many people trying to join the team. The rest of the organization would also be more than willing to help my team reach our objectives.

His advice has served me well, but beyond the need to share glory and recognition, I have always been both humbled and thrilled when one of my people takes an idea or assignment and turns it into something great. Their achievement is almost always beyond what I might have done myself, and so it is easy for me to want to feature their great work. My reward is having a great team that accomplishes great things!

Building a culture of caring and compassion takes time, effort, and intention.

Questions to Consider

- How does your organization exhibit a culture of caring?
- How can your organization make a habit of expressing gratitude?
- How does (or can) your leadership work to reduce selfishness in your organization?

Notes

1. Dutton, J. E., Lilius, J. M., & Kanov, J. M. (2007). The transformative potential of compassion at work. *Handbook of Transformative Cooperation: New Designs and Dynamics, 1,* 107–126.
2. Ibid.
3. Seppälä, E., & Cameron, K. (2015). Proof that positive work cultures are more productive. *Harvard Business Review, 12*(1), 44–50.
4. http://www.rhinofoods.eom/stuff/contentmgr/files/l/f06979adb30aad81d-139a595b01ad0b0/download/guide___working_bridges_version_3_15_11.pdf
5. Pascale, R. (1990). *Managing on the edge: How the smartest companies use conflict to stay ahead.* New York, NY: Simon & Schuster.
6. http://www.industryweek.com/articles/cutting_costs_without_cutting_peo-ple_24095.aspx?ShowAll=1&SectionID=3

20 RENEWING CULTURE BY REBUILDING TRUST

In the 1990s, scores of GM employees who had lost their jobs at other GM plants that had closed were transferring to the Parma organization. Bob and his executive team created a one-week training program for these transfers to socialize them into Parma's culture and its team-based approach, and to minimize the potential for a recreation of the dysfunctional cultures of the plants they had left. Socializing them was difficult because of their hostility. They certainly did not come to Parma with a positive attitude. They were angry that their previous organization had failed and transferred them. They also were unfamiliar with working in teams. Finally, they had had to uproot their families and move, often hundreds of miles, in order to retain their jobs, albeit highly paid ones.

One day, Bob was walking through the plant and came to where a new operation was being set up and one of the transferees.

> Because I didn't know this particular guy, I asked him about his work. He said to me, "Hey, aren't you the plant manager?" I replied, "Yes, I am." He then says, "This place is horrible (he used far more colorful language)! I'll tell you how we did it at my old plant. We would never do this kind of crap there (again, a more colorful term was used)." He went on and on about how this was a terrible place, that he was mad that he had been transferred here, and that he wanted to get out if he could.

> After letting him say his piece, I said, "Well, I'm sorry if you feel that way, but you'll find out it's a pretty good place to work." He said, "Bullshit, I hate it here." I replied, "I hope you don't go home and take this [kind of attitude] out to your family, because you are one unhappy individual." I then left him to go to my next meeting.

> Several weeks later, we began recruiting new employees, as there were no longer any more laid-off GM employees to rehire from closed-down plants. Because of the enormous demand for these jobs, we implemented a process that gave each of our existing employees one employment application that they could then give to a family member or friend who wanted to work at Parma. Employees could pick up their application after their shift ended.

DOI: 10.4324/9780367822170-24

As I headed to a meeting, I walked past the line of employees waiting to receive their application, and I see this guy standing in the line. The same guy who'd chewed me out several weeks before. I didn't want to be late for my meeting, and so I kept walking.

But I just had to find out—who in the hell would this guy want to get a job for, because he'd called it such a terrible place? When I walked back toward him, he immediately turned his back on me and tried to find a crack in the wall in which to hide. I wasn't going to let him off so easily, and so I tapped him on the shoulder. "I'm surprised you're here to get an application for somebody to work at this terrible place. That's just awful. You'd said you wouldn't want anyone to work here. Well, who do you want to hurt so badly by getting them a job here?" I asked.

He gave his answer in a low voice. I'd clearly heard what he said but wanted him to know for sure I'd heard it, so I said, "I didn't hear your answer." He replied again, this time with his hand over his mouth. Again, I said, "I don't think I heard that." Finally, in a normal voice, he says, "It's for my son."

We develop trust with others over time based on our experiences with them.[1] Positive experiences reinforce our trusting beliefs, and trust grows. With negative experiences, our level of trust is typically reevaluated. We either decrease trust in specific areas or decrease our overall level of trust.[2,3,4] Distrust, then, is not the absence of trust, but rather an expectation that another will not act in a trustworthy manner, based on our previous interactions with that party.[5] Trust that has been created can also be broken, and it happens at work more often than we think: Someone takes credit for our ideas; someone turns in their part of a project later than expected; or someone uses harsher words than they realized.

One of Karen's MBA students, Daniel Quinn, shared how he rebuilt trust while working in the military in a civilian role.

I had to overcome a lot of distrust when I became the accounting operations chief for the DOD [Department of Defense]. I was the first person ever to be hired off the street to a senior-level position into the USPFO [United States Property and Fiscal Office]. No one trusted anything I said because I was an outsider. Once I proved my competence, however, people then thought I was an internal spy, sent from another agency. It did not help that, eight months into my role, I had already busted a travel expense scheme that sent three individuals to jail and was working with the Department of Justice on tracking a foreign agent selling goods to China. That really was not what I went there for! People eventually realized I was there to work hard and make the organization better. I'm still friends with many of the people I worked with.

If both parties are not willing to repair the broken trust, then it simply will not happen. If both parties are willing to repair the trust violation, however, then direct approaches will have greater success in rebuilding trust.[6] Rebuilding trust involves both parties attempting to resolve discrepancies in their belief as to what caused the trust to be broken in the first place.[7]

Research on rebuilding trust has found that apologies work best if the trust breach appears to be an isolated event.[8] First, the one whose trust has been broken must have the courage to share what happened. This is not always easy because we fear reprisal or misunderstanding. Then, the person who broke our trust must be humble enough to acknowledge the wrongdoing or mistake, apologize for it, and promise that it will be corrected. This act may begin to repair and rebuild trust.[9] If the person is a leader, all of this must be done in a visible, even public, fashion.

The Reverend Jim Wenger, pastor of St. John Lutheran Church in Deshler, Ohio shared his perspective on apologies:

> The maturity to say we are truly sorry and to take responsibility for our own mistakes doesn't come easily. The temptation to save face and blame someone else or to blame circumstances is an easy way out. But if there is a misunderstanding, if there have been hard feelings, taking ownership of how our own actions may have contributed to the misunderstanding immediately lessens the defensiveness that leaves people divided and on opposite sides.

Apologies are not sufficient for trust repair, however.[10] Following any apology, the behavior of the trust violator obviously should be consistent with the apology.[11] To truly repair trust, the violator must understand how trust came to be violated in the first place.[12] This requires the violator to ask the victim what is necessary from their perspective to repair the trust. Asking, "How can I make this up to you?" is a good start.

In his work on positive leaders, Kim Cameron has found that such leaders encourage other members of the organization to not only express gratitude and compassion in their relationships with others, but forgiveness as well.[13] This is crucial. Rebuilding trust is exceedingly difficult because although the offending party may apologize in an effort to restore broken trust, restoring the relationship requires the aggrieved party to be willing to forgive.

In one of our recent workshops on how to rebuild trust, we learned that it was much easier for people to think of instances where their trust had been broken than where they had broken someone else's trust. The group agreed that it was probably because a) no one had taken the time or had the courage to tell them that they had been untrustworthy, or b) we tend to think that we do not do things to break the trust of others. In many instances, then, broken trust at work is *unintentional*. Somebody said or did something *without realizing* that their words or actions violated the other's trust.

If broken trust is unintentional, how can we be more intentional about restoring such trust? One way is to explicitly state how our trust has been broken, focusing on the facts rather than how they have made us feel. It takes courage to be open and honest, but it will save time and, ideally, the relationship. Sometimes trust is broken because the leader is unaware of how the change effort is affecting people in the organization. Aneil's college friend Hal Stern described what happens when leaders do not show that they care:

> One of the more personal and painful experiences for me was during a rather difficult local crisis, and a particular leader in my organization did not check up on me or my peers during the event or its aftermath. Eighteen months later, I was doubtful the same leader would protect my interests during a reorganization, and I was proven correct. It's the final "C" in ROCC—Caring— that would have pushed through this issue, and I felt that without the caring I tended to trust other ostensible "employee outreach" efforts a bit less.

Once again, to be intentional means you need to be proactive and not assume that people will come to you, especially in a crisis. As illustrated in Figure 20.1 (Mishra & Mishra, 2022), here is a checklist to use when you consider rebuilding trust, whether it is your responsibility to do so or not.

At the organizational level, previous research has shown that stakeholders are more likely to forgive an organization that already possesses a high level of trustworthiness with its stakeholders.[14] In addition, researchers have documented how trust within organizations typically suffers during a crisis.[15] It is critical, then, for leaders to build a culture of trust before a crisis occurs, especially because the innovative behavior that will enable the organization to resolve the crisis depends upon mutual trust within that organization. If trust is sufficiently low before the crisis, then the organization will typically default

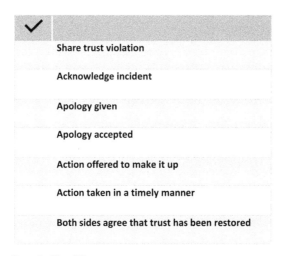

Figure 20.1 Trust Repair Checklist

to practices and behaviors that are no longer effective and indeed may have contributed to the crisis. This logic applies to relationships between the organization and its external stakeholders as well. If mutual trust has been built with customers and suppliers, that will promote flexible, creative responses that lead to crisis resolution.

Mike Gannon shares how he was able to rebuild trust at one division where he worked:

> During the Great Recession (between 2007 and 2009), I worked for a division of a major, tier-one auto supplier. Unfortunately, the parent company declared bankruptcy and decided that our division should be closed because of our heavy losses and a large number of high-wage hourly employees in both western Europe and in the USA.
>
> Our division asked for the opportunity to restructure and sell it to another company or investor. While the odds were firmly stacked against us, we had exciting new technology in the pipeline and an outstanding workforce. We were also blessed with an extraordinary CEO who instinctively understood the ROCC of Trust. As a result, he and I had developed a large reservoir of trust with our global workforce.
>
> During the restructuring process, we faced incredible challenges, ever-changing demands, and countless setbacks. The story of our transformation process would have made a fascinating reality TV show, except nobody would have believed all that we went through. During our transformation process we continued to measure employee engagement. Our scores continued to improve and were among the highest recorded by our survey company. More importantly, we saved the division, and it is now a very successful, independent company.
>
> So how did we do it? Trust! A good example of this was our extensive communication process. The CEO strongly believed that if people all had the same information, employees could use their judgment to make good decisions on the spot.
>
> Every month, we had an information update for all of our global supervisors and above. The CEO would openly share the developments of the past month. When I say openly, I mean *openly*! He shared his fears and concerns. He shared confidential information that would have caused big issues if it had leaked (it never did) and he always explained a pathway to success … even if it seemed to have low odds for success.
>
> This was especially important for our survival because we needed our automotive customers to award us new business, and we knew

that would not happen if our customers sensed we might not be around to serve them. We knew that the key to maintaining customer confidence was the daily interactions customers had with our engineers and plant staff. Because our global team was so well informed and engaged, our customers stuck with us through thick and thin.

The method we used to address high labor costs at our most significant location is another powerful example of trust being the foundation for success. The union leadership knew that the location was making huge losses and trusted that our senior management wanted to save the location (at that time, similar locations at other companies were being closed). The CEO pledged a total "open book" approach on all the information regarding the plant. He invited the union to engage their top experts to study our books, and said he did not care "how the pie was sliced," so long as the plant was viable in the end.

We were blessed with a courageous and savvy union leadership team, and together we fashioned the plan that saved the plant. It was difficult and took sacrifices by all parties, but because of the trust relationship on both sides, we were able to bridge great difficulties. Today, the plant continues to be successful.

Rebuilding a culture of trust also takes intention to ensure that not only is trust being rebuilt, but that important relationships are restored as well. Ariel Investments co-CEO John Rogers Jr. provided this example:

When I was on the board at the University of Chicago Laboratory Schools, a private school, the teachers had a union. There was a lot of distrust between the teachers and the administration following a tough contract negotiation. I remember saying, "Our teachers are our most valuable assets. They're in the classrooms every day with our students. What they've done based upon their union contract is perfectly legal and appropriate. So, some people can be angry with them for arbitrating this or challenging that, but there's no upside for staying angry with them for executing their lawful rights as a union."

When I got to be chairman of the board of the Lab School, the first thing that I did was nominate to our board of directors a former, well-respected teacher who'd won the Golden Apple award, and who had had been an extraordinary part of the Lab School faculty and a parent of Lab School students. She's a brilliant woman, a tough woman: smart, thoughtful, and caring. This was first time we had someone from the faculty on the board. I was to try to rebuild trust between the union leadership and the administration.

She was fabulous. She was just the right thing to do to rebuild that trust.

We spent a lot of time building closer personal relationships with the teachers and with union leadership. We had the president of the University of Chicago involved in building those connections, having him spend his valuable time nurturing those relationships with key teachers ... key educational leaders at the Lab School. I think we did a lot to rebuild the trust between the faculty and the administration.

Questions to Consider

- What have been the results when a leader has failed to rebuild trust?
- What are some areas in your organization that need to have trust rebuilt?
- What have been the results of any efforts by your organization to rebuild trust?

Notes

1. Tomlinson, E. C., & Mayer, R. C. (2009). The role of causal attribution dimension in trust repair. *Academy of Management Review, 34*(1), 85–104.
2. Lewicki, R. J., Tomlinson, E. C., & Gillespie, N. (2006). Models of interpersonal trust development: Theoretical approaches, empirical evidence, and future directions. *Journal of Management, 32*(6), 991–1022.
3. Janowicz-Panjaitan, J., & Krishan, R. (2009). Measures for dealing with competence and integrity violations of interorganizational trust at the corporate and operating levels of organizational hierarchy. *Journal of Management Studies, 46*(2), 245–268.
4. Lewicki, R., Elgoibar, P., & Euwema, M. (Eds.) (2016). The tree of trust: Building and repairing trust in organizations. In *Building trust and constructive conflict management in organizations* (pp. 93–117). Springer, Cham.
5. Lewicki, R. J., & Wiethoff, C. (2000). Trust, trust development, and trust repair. In M. Deutsch, & P. T. Coleman (Eds.), *The handbook of conflict resolution: Theory and practice* (pp. 86–107). Jossey-Bass.
6. Lewicki, R. J., & Wiethoff, C. (2000). Trust, trust development, and trust repair. In M. Deutsch, & P. T. Coleman (Eds.), *The handbook of conflict resolution: Theory and practice* (pp. 86–107). Jossey-Bass.
7. Lewicki, R. J., & Wiethoff, C. (2000). Trust, trust development, and trust repair. In M. Deutsch, & P. T. Coleman (Eds.), *The handbook of conflict resolution: Theory and practice* (pp. 86–107). Jossey-Bass.
8. Tomlinson, E., Dineen, B., & Lewicki, R. (2004). The road to reconciliation: Antecedents of victim willingness to reconcile following a broken promise. *Journal of Management, 30*(2), 165–187.
9. Frost, P. (2003). *Toxic emotions at work: How compassionate managers handle pain and conflict.* Harvard Business School Press.

10. Ferrin, D. L., Kim, P. H., Cooper, C. D., & Dirks, K. T. (2007). Silence speaks volumes: The effectiveness of reticence in comparison to apology and denial for responding to integrity- and competence-based trust violations. *Journal of Applied Psychology, 92*(4), 893–908.
11. Hui, C. H., Lau, F. L. Y., Tsang, L., & Pak, S. (2011). The impact of post-apology behavioral consistency on victim's forgiveness intention: A study of trust violation among coworkers. *Journal of Applied Social Psychology, 41*(5), 1214–1236.
12. Schoorman, F. D., Mayer, R. C., & David, J. H. (2007). An integrative model of organizational trust: Past, present, and future. *The Academy of Management Review, 32*(2), 344–354.
13. Cameron, K. (2012). *Positive leadership: Strategies for extraordinary performance.* Berrett-Koehler Publishers.
14. Coombs, W. T. (1999). Information and compassion in crisis responses: A test of their effects. *Journal of Public Relations Research, 11*(2), 125–143.
15. Gillespie, N., Searle, R., Gustafsson, S. & Hailey, V. H. (2020). Preserving employee trust during crisis. *Behavioral Science and Policy, 6*(COVID-19 special issue), 1–10.

21
CREATING A DIVERSE, EQUITABLE, AND INCLUSIVE CULTURE

Bob had just sat down with a team during one of its regular meetings. The team's area of responsibility involved challenging, physically hard work. One of the female staff members talked about how she just could not keep up with the work. She had been doing it for three weeks, going home very sore, and she could not do it anymore. She told Bob, "I can't do it anymore, and nobody cares in my group."

One of her team members then blurted out, "Well, you have to pay your dues like we did, you know. You're nothing special." Bob's comment back was, "Let me just ask you this question: If this were your daughter, would you want your daughter to do that for eight hours a day, day after day?" The guy had a real sheepish look on his face, and he responded, "No. No."

Bob called these incidents significant emotional events, which not only touched him deeply, and the staff member who shared her experience, but also the colleague who was so critical of her. Bob could see in their eyes that people began looking at things in a totally different manner as a result just "one little conversation." Bob himself wondered how many times he'd treated his own peers poorly. Bob also learned that the understanding those conversations created not only permeated throughout the workforce, but through to the union leadership as well.

Previous research on diversity, equity, and inclusion, or DEI, has found that when organizations openly address DEI concerns, as Bob did regarding the female employee, trust is built and employee engagement improves.[1] In addition, when leaders make DEI a priority, employees see that their leaders support workplace diversity and their trust in their leader also improves.[2]

John Rogers Jr. is setting an example inside his firm, Ariel Investments, and in working with other organizations:

> The Ariel Community Academy and the work we've done around financial literacy will, we hope, be a model for how financial institutions can partner with urban public schools, and is something we're really proud of. Then, the newest program at the University of Chicago that we've supported financially is the creation of a program for minority students to have summer internships in the investment offices of major endowments, exposing them to financial services careers. Initially, we've had 18 students placed all over the country in various endowments, and we think we'll get up to 40 relatively soon.

DOI: 10.4324/9780367822170-25

Finally, [co-CEO] Melody and I are fortunate to be on corporate boards where we are trying to get them to do the right thing. We're pushing the majority companies to have minority partners and executives. I know Melody has done similar work at boards she sits on. It's one thing to have impact from our small Ariel place, but you can have so much impact when you're sitting on a corporate board and getting them to think about these issues in a progressive way. Over 55 times over the years at Ariel, we've been able to encourage companies to appoint diverse board members.

Being diverse, equitable, and inclusive means thinking about these concepts broadly and deeply. In addition to including underrepresented groups, it also means looking to including those whose disabilities and disadvantages are not as visible or readily identifiable yet are still significant. In addition, it is not enough to say that we want a diverse workforce without actively and intentionally making it happen. Then, once we have hired the people who make our organization better, we need to actively help them to feel included and that they belong. One of Karen's Wake Forest University alumni, Tom Tymann, described DEI this way:

> Promoting diversity, equity, and inclusion means giving someone a chance based on their passion and hard work instead of what their title or history is. By valuing the opinions of their team members, an effective leader will instill a sense of worth in them that will result in organizational growth.

As with most important issues, creating a diverse, equitable, and inclusive culture requires that leaders first listen. Aneil's former graduate assistant Samantha Pittman described what works in her organization:

> Our organization has first and foremost listened to those diverse voices and determined what was important to *them*. What may seem like a step forward to some isn't actually the inclusion the diverse community is looking for. We need to avoid assuming we know what one another needs or wants and *listen*.

The former Chairman and CEO of Turkish Airlines Dr. Cem Kozlu whom Aneil first met while he was conducting leadership development programs with Coca-Cola İçecek in Istanbul, described how his company improved DEI:

> The most effective practices to improve diversity, equity, and inclusion in my experience require including deserving women in the team, promoting young talent, and bringing in outside talent, thus creating an effective mix.

Aneil's former MBA student, Juan Carlos Sanchez, broadens the meaning of DEI to include diversity of thought:

> DEI is the topic of the decade, and it lost its meaning with so much in the way of politics and agendas behind it. Real diversity, equity, and inclusion don't relate to the color of the skin, background, etc. It really is the diversity of thought, and as such I think I have not truly seen full diversity and inclusion.

Our former WFU colleague Kellie Sauls emphasized the role that leaders have in sharing responsibility for improving DEI:

> Improving diversity and equity and including inclusion requires leaders to emphasize our shared responsibility for these. DEI impacts all areas of an organization, so all need to be in the habit of thinking about it, discussing it, and making decisions in light of it. Providing training on how to do that well is instrumental.

Promoting true DEI begins with developing a pipeline of diverse talent. Chris Deshazor described how he opened up the hiring pipeline at one of his former firms to ensure a more diverse set of candidates:

> What are we doing to organically build up our diverse talent, whether they are folks who are fresh out of college or have been in their career for 10 years? How do we build these folks up?

> When I was hiring Megan almost a year and a half ago, I started with 480 resumes for that position. The system went through and eliminated a lot them based on whether they had certain requirements. For this position, a college degree was required. If they didn't have a college degree listed, the system automatically booted them out. So, I went through those 480 resumes myself, and culled it down to 20. Then my recruiter did screenings on those 20.

> My final six included an African American male and an African American female. I had a former teacher. I had a person who was a manager at a grocery store. It was a different vibe. I had very diverse candidates. But the most important thing was, rather than race, we had candidates who had very different types of skill sets.

> I didn't know it at the time, but Megan was of mixed Honduran and White heritage. She's been a rock star. She is a rock star. I knew that she was Honduran, but I didn't know that she spoke Spanish. There was a particular situation which I was dealing with in Mexico. I needed to roll out a program there. As we're getting feedback about how to do the program, Megan says, "In Latin American culture, giving feedback is a little bit harder for women."

I didn't know that, and so we had a conversation about it. I did a little more research, and realized she was spot-on. So, we totally changed the way the program was implemented. Normally we would go in and say, "Hey, everybody, give us feedback, give feedback on your peers." Instead, we did a more interactive feedback session. We used QR codes, had people take it on their phones, and give feedback anonymously.

Feedback on that program in Mexico was through the roof. Having her knowledge was very beneficial. Had it just been me, I wouldn't have known that and the project probably wouldn't have gone over as well.

To promote true DEI, an organization needs to provide training that is substantial, hold deeply authentic conversations, and have a strong mentoring program. Chris also shared how his former employer is now providing DEI training that he hopes will be more enduring and impactful:

A lot of people look at DEI as something to just get through. It's one hour or two hours, or a half-day or full-day class. Just take this class and now go back and you are DEI certified, and you are great. People go in, they do it, but they go back to their same old habits.

Ours is a six-module, nine-week program. The first week involves watching a video about a set topic, in this case, inclusion, who you are, and understanding yourself. The second week, you come in and discuss the conversations you've been having about DEI. If you're a manager, did you talk to folks on your team? Did you talk to other managers? If you're an individual contributor, did you have a conversation? It's pushing people to have conversations. Week three, another set of conversations. Week four, new topic.

The goal is to keep people talking about these things and building on them. By the time you get to week nine and we've gone through all of the topics, then we host a learning circle where we bring folks together. What's different? How did this change for you? What was difficult? What went really well? These learning circles bring a lot of things out.

Right after George Floyd was killed, we held a forum involving several African Americans from around the company, and it was very moving. We called it a "daring dialogue." It went over really well.

Since then, all our executives have mentees. I started mentoring folks myself and I have three right now. I was very hesitant at first, because I'm, like, "Why are you asking me to be a mentor? I'm not a mentor. I'm just Chris." In working with them, it's been more about giving ideas. It's having conversations. I love the fact that they want to bounce something off of me. I do this myself with my own long-standing mentor, Tim.

LISA'S LIFE AS A DEI LEADER

Our sister Dr. Lisa Repaskey died unexpectedly from a pulmonary embolism over Memorial Weekend in 2021. This book is dedicated to her memory because she was truly the most inclusive leader in our family, long before it was in the business lexicon. She became a godmother to a baby from Nigeria as a high-school senior, and this event influenced her throughout her life. She chose to do her student teaching in Spanish Harlem in New York City and came home from that experience wearing a "Free Nelson Mandela" bracelet, and determined to make a difference in her own way.

She then set out to work in Oakland, California determined that her kindergarten class, where more than 10 languages were spoken, would all know how to read English before the end of the year. From there, she went on to earn a Ph.D. in literacy, so that she could help new teachers learn how to teach reading to inner-city children. She taught at a historically Black college and university (HBCU), where she improved student outcomes in their end-of-year exams during her short time there. She mentored a young man, buying his textbooks as well as clothing for interviews, because she believed that there needed to be more Black men teaching elementary school.

Lisa led with purpose and by example. She did not just say that things should be diverse, equitable, and inclusive; she lived her life that way. She built a culture of trust among her students, parents, college students, and colleagues, which showed them what was truly important, not just by her words, but also by her actions.

Questions to Consider

- Is there a sufficient culture of trust to have honest conversations about DEI in your organization?
- What substantive practices in your organization exist to reinforce DEI?
- Is there one person in your organization whom you could get to know to enhance DEI?

Notes

1 Downey, S. N., van der Werff, L., Thomas, K. M., & Plaut, V. C. (2015). The role of diversity practices and inclusion in promoting trust and employee engagement. *Journal of Applied Social Psychology*, 45(1), 35–44.
2 Goswami, S., & Goswami, B. K. (2018). Exploring the relationship between workforce diversity, inclusion and employee engagement. *Drishtikon: A Management Journal*, 9(1), 65–89.

PART IV

LEADERSHIP THAT LASTS

22

LEADERSHIP **THAT** LASTS

Finally, a culture of trust is not valuable unless it is an enduring culture. We show how our trustworthy leaders have worked hard to build cultures that have thrived long after their own tenures, by using proper succession planning, setting rigorous metrics, and laying the foundations for lasting results. In addition, we encourage our readers to enlarge their purpose by using their strengths, talents, and abilities to help build something larger than themselves, whether it be with their community or the world.

As part of Bob and Parma's plans to engage everyone, unionized hourly employees, salaried employees, and managers took on increasing responsibility for quality and process improvement processes. They were dedicated to helping the plant succeed and were fully accountable for their results. Roles that had previously been reserved for managers were now being given to hourly employees. Hourly employees were given the role of quality coordinator for each area or zone of the plant. This coordinator role included gathering data on quality and producing the charts that all teams in each particular zone relied upon as part of their daily work.

On two or three occasions, one of these hourly quality coordinators stopped by to tell Bob how much he enjoyed his work and being included in helping the Parma plant "move forward." Then, just before Christmas of that year, this coordinator died of a heart attack, despite being in his early fifties. After Christmas, his wife called Bob and introduced herself. She talked about how hard it had been to lose him and how it was even harder for it to have happened at that time of the year. She just wanted Bob to know, however, how significantly Parma's cultural change had improved how her late husband had felt about himself and how he felt about his family.

She went on to say that everything at home had become much more positive. Her husband would come home every night from work with a manila folder full of all kinds of charts and reports. He would then work on them for two or three hours to get ready for the next day. Three years prior to his death, the family had given him a briefcase for Christmas. His wife said going to work carrying a briefcase was like adding another notch on his self-esteem belt.

In our opinion, for an hourly employee to be working two to three hours without being paid was testimony to just how dramatically the culture at Parma had changed under Bob's leadership.

DOI: 10.4324/9780367822170-27

The effort to build a culture of trust at Parma not only resulted in significant performance improvements during Bob's tenure at the plant, but also in the more than two decades since he retired in 1999. Machine efficiency more than doubled while Bob was the plant manager, and then increased another 50% over the decade following his retirement, to where it is now equal to the best stamping plants in the world. Labor productivity more than quadrupled while he led the Parma plant, and more than doubled again in the following decade, to where this is also now at world-class levels even as annual revenue quadrupled to more than $1 billion. In addition, tens of millions of dollars in cost savings each year have been achieved. As a result of its performance, General Motors has invested hundreds of millions of dollars in the plant since 2016, including over $40 million announced at the end of 2021.[1]

Improvements in quality were even more dramatic, increasing several hundred-fold under Bob's leadership. The cost of all of the training to improve employee engagement and accountability was paying off. One number that Bob was particularly proud of was getting their defects to less than six parts per million, which was world class and is continuing to improve. Most importantly, Bob, his leadership team, the Shop Committee run by the hourly employees, and the local UAW leaders helped to save thousands of high-paying jobs as GM shut down stamping plant after stamping plant over the course of three decades.

Karen's former colleague, Dr. Anitra Manning, shared with us how she is currently enlarging her purpose in her current role at IBM.

I received powerful advice from Frances Hesselbein years ago: be so good at what you do, that you'll never have to interview again. Although her sentiments speak of her journey, I nonetheless have understood her advice to be about doing good work that makes it easy for me to tell wholehearted impact stories. I have also been gifted with understanding when it is time to move forward. I have been a part of large-scale corporate transformations and financial crises that resulted in job loss. I got through those dry seasons—because job loss can be profoundly traumatic as it is rife with vocational questioning—by changing how I saw those moments. Once I realized that I completed my assignment in those roles, new ones—jobs of my dreams could and did come to me. My last two leadership roles came as a result of me saying years earlier: "that seems like a great organization. I'd love to work there one day."

My current role came to me as I began considering ways that I could be more impactful in supporting empathetic, ethical, and inclusive organizational cultures. I truly believe that the workplace cultivates individual wholeness and the individual's wholeness expands to families, communities, and nations. That is the impact that I hope that I'll make at work. As I was thinking about this possibility in the midst of what felt like socially painful times (murders of three

Black Americans, one who was fellow Gen Xer), my sponsors were speaking about me in rooms that I was not in, concluding with me launching my current role in the summer of 2021. I am here now because of an openness to see a different perspective—how I might contribute. Once I did, new choices could unfold.

I am honored to manage the operational work of OneTen Raleigh-Durham market on behalf of IBM. I am inspired by OneTen's goal of developing a skills-first economy and leveraging that intended reality to hire and mobilize one million Black talent into family-sustaining jobs within ten years. It is exciting to work with corporate partners and community friends in service of this impactful goal. I am also responsible for consulting our Americas markets in strengthening our inclusive culture. As the Americas D&I Strategy and Programs Leader, I contribute to enabling an inclusive workplace across the Americas region. Good and meaningful work is important. In this role, I am able to leverage my talent management and development skills and strengths to advance equity at-scale. I love to multiply good and believe that IBM is a catalyst for so much good.

Even while operating and growing as a for-profit business, Ted Castle and Rhino Foods sought to be known as a company focused on the well-being of their employees and the community. As Ted says:

I'm a person that learns by looking, watching, reading, thinking, trying. So, I read about business, listen to podcasts about business, talk to people about business. That's why I got totally into becoming a B Corp. Rhino's purpose is to impact the manner in which business is done and the B Corp mission is business as a force for good. One of the biggest reasons I'm part of the B Corps movement is to be around other great business leaders and learn from them.

For all leaders, there comes a time to pass the baton to the next generation of leaders. We asked local North Carolina Two Men and a Truck, Inc. franchisee Brooke Wilson: "When do you know it is time to leave an organization, or step down as its leader?" Her response was to say:

When the passion isn't there anymore, or when there is an inability to lead. My objective is to continue to develop leaders and create opportunities for the people on my team. We routinely celebrate the successes of our business in incentive programs, retreats, and awards. As a married partnership without children to contribute long-term investment to, we are currently working with legal advisers to develop a profit-sharing and equity plan for our tenured team members. This plan will include all long-term contributors to the team—not just director or C suite levels (like most organizations). We recognize that our frontline teams are the backbone of our organization and tend to be those that will be most impacted by such agreements. In addition, every team needs its "followers," and without these contributors, we would not have experienced the successes we have. When I'm ready to get out of the business, I hope to leave with an expression of gratitude and opportunity towards those who have been committed and have contributed over the years.

Leaving a lasting legacy is one way to ensure that the leadership initiatives you have put in place will remain long after you leave.

Questions to Consider

- What would people say are the most important lasting results that your organization has achieved (or should achieve)?
- Do you have leadership development and/or succession planning in place to ensure that the results will last?
- What is one thing you want to be remembered for as a leader?

Note

1. https://gmauthority.com/blog/2021/11/general-motors-to-invest-46m-in-parma-ohio-metal-stamping-plant/

23

ENLARGING **YOUR** PURPOSE

Bob and the Cleveland Clinic

Bob Lintz got deeply involved serving the greater Cleveland community while he was still at GM. He chaired or served as a board member to numerous charitable, civic, and educational organizations. GM had always been supportive of community needs and Bob felt that giving back was an important component to building his own character. In fact, he still feels strongly that young leaders should get involved in giving back to their communities. It is a way to learn from other outstanding leaders and to understand more about the community in which you live and work. As Bob says, "Giving back can be as rewarding as doing your own job."

Bob became deeply involved with the Cleveland Clinic after they successfully treated his kidney cancer discovered during a routine checkup. As he got to know the leaders there better, they invited him to join the clinic's board of trustees in 1991, where he continues to serve to this day.

Bob's experience in employee engagement and quality improvement have been very helpful to the Cleveland Clinic, which has been very focused on improving patient experience with caregivers and service quality. Bob has been able to share his experience and expertise with the clinic by serving on the board's Audit, Research and Education, and Safety, Quality, and Patient Experience committees.[1] Employees of the Cleveland Clinic have also toured the Parma plant to learn more about GM's approach to teamwork and meeting and exceeding customers' expectations. When we asked him why he still spends so much time volunteering as a trustee, Bob replied, "If they feel I'm contributing, I will continue to serve. I can't stop caring."

The leaders we have profiled here live by a different set of values and rules, enlarging their purpose to one that goes beyond just returning profits to shareholders or their own bottom line. These leaders have enlarged their purpose by "associating with a cause in order to give purpose to [their] lives," drawing on communities of stakeholders for inspiration. As business scholar Charles Handy points out, these kinds of leader measure success "in terms of outcomes for others"[2] as well as for themselves.

Harvard Business School Professor Rosabeth Moss Kanter has argued that when a private company engages in a partnership with the public sector, the result can be solutions to real community problems while providing employees with renewed energy in their current jobs.[3] Ted Castle of Rhino Foods has demonstrated a great example of this in partnering with several public service and nonprofit organizations in Vermont. He and his company

DOI: 10.4324/9780367822170-28

have also worked hard to integrate refugees from Bosnia and several African countries, first by teaching them English as a second language, followed by the "language of business" that all Rhino Foods employees are trained in, so that they can help contribute equally to key decisions made by the company. As *UVM Today*, the University of Vermont news for employees, students, and alumni wrote, these "New Americans now represent 30 to 40 percent of Rhino's employees."[4] As Ted Castle shared with us:

> We have gotten very focused on hiring refugees. Burlington is an area where refugees are being resettled, and we'd begun hiring Bosnian refugees since the late '90s. Now we have many refugees from all over the world, roughly 30% of our workforce is composed of refugees. Vermont is not a diverse place like other parts of the country, so we look at increasing diversity as a good thing for our business. We think it makes us a stronger company.

> This isn't really a story about me. It's a story about us realizing that we have English language learners at Rhino. We are an open book company and share so much information within our company. We want our workers to think and act like owners. As we started teaching English, there were some real challenges, but now that we've worked ourselves through it, we look at this as a really powerful engine to our company.

> We have some amazing people working here. We work on creating a relationship with our people where it is ok to speak up and tell us how we can be a better company.

One other way to enlarge your purpose is to mentor others, whether they are in your organization or outside of it. We asked North Carolina-based Two Men and a Truck franchisee Brooke Wilson about how she has mentored others beyond her organization:

> I have mentored other persons—whether inside my organization or out. I have supported employees' initiatives to become independent entrepreneurs through training and lending advice or investing in them financially. I seek opportunities every day to provide a positive influence on someone, which may be as simple as coaching a frontline employee.

> In the early years of managing my first Two Men and a Truck [TMT] franchise, I was highly engaged with the frontline staff as an owner–operator of the business. There are a number of examples in which I aided employees' development outside of the organization. I helped an employee learn English. I helped an employee with financial coaching, so that he could budget and eventually purchase his own home.

On a larger scale, Les and I have helped committed managers purchase their own franchise within the brand and within other non-competing brands. Brian and Tim's purchase of the Greenville, North Carolina franchise was probably the first significant example. Rich Rivera, a long-term team member, recently signed a franchise agreement with TMT, International, and the franchise opened in Goldsboro, North Carolina in 2021. A former regional manager just moved to Las Vegas, Nevada and signed an agreement with the Clean Eatz franchise. Jonathan Cuttino, our Georgia regional manager, is opening a TMT franchise in Macon, Georgia, in March 2022. Another success story of moving a manager forward within our TMT system!

You do not have to wait until the end of your career to consider how you can enlarge your purpose. You have all the tools and capabilities with you now to give back to your community in ways that enrich others. We hope that this advice from our trustworthy leaders will help you on your own journey to becoming a trusted leader. We look forward to hearing from you as you make your own leadership more intentional.

Questions to Consider

- How do you encourage and support your employees to share their leadership capabilities with the communities you serve?
- Who do you envision as future partners from the community to solve critical issues in the community?
- How can you extend your leadership beyond your organization?

Notes

1. Cleveland Clinic. (n.d.) *Board of trustees.* http://my.clevelandclinic.org/about-cleveland-clinic/overview/leadership/board-of-trustees.aspx
2. Handy, C. (2002, December 1). What's a business for? *Harvard Business Review,* 8.
3. Kanter, R. M. (1999). From spare change to real change: The social sector as beta site for business innovation. *Harvard Business Review, 77*(3), 122–132.
4. Catania, K. (2021, November 4).*The scoop on cookie dough ice cream.* UVM Today. https://www.uvm.edu/news/story/scoop-cookie-dough-ice-cream?utm_source=Facebook.com&utm_medium=post&utm_term&utm_content&utm_campaign=uvmmagazine-fall21&fbclid=IwAR0kFV18QuuA1DHjvQ5nof_kaKUlLtjbteTLx-nAhZsUqAq1O4Ldt4Z8oew

APPENDIX 1: LEADER BIOGRAPHIES

Dr. Karen Mishra

Dr. Karen Mishra teaches marketing and management in the Lundy–Fetterman School of Business at Campbell University in Buies Creek, North Carolina. She also teaches leadership in the American Bankers Association (ABA) Stonier Graduate School of Banking at Wharton (University of Pennsylvania) and is the co-author of two books on trustworthy leadership. She serves on the board of Preston's League, a Durham nonprofit which serves children and families on the pediatric bone marrow transplant floor at Duke Hospital.

Karen's research focuses on how companies use internal marketing to share and extend the mission of their organizations as well as to build trust and engagement with employees. She has worked with both SAS and Lenovo to understand the nuances of internal communication within a global organization in a digital world. Her research has been published in publications such as *International Journal of Business Communication*, the *Handbook of Effective Communication, Leadership, and Conflict Resolution*, and *Sloan Management Review*.

Karen provides marketing planning, sales training, leadership development, and executive coaching for Fortune 500 and start-up companies. She has created and implemented strategic marketing plans for nonprofits and start-ups, including Michigan State University, Wake Forest University, the Innovatrium, and Point Dx, a digital radiology firm. She served as chief marketing officer for a healthcare analytics start-up during its founding year and has been an executive coach through Duke Corporate Education. In addition to her two books on leadership with co-author Dr. Aneil Mishra she most recently contributed a chapter on using StrengthsFinder 2.0 with MBAs to a book on restoring trust in higher education. She is also the co-author of *A Beginner's Guide to Mobile Marketing* with Dole digital executive Molly Garris. She is a certified Global Gallup Strengths coach.

Karen has a B.A. in Economics and Music from Albion College. After working for the Oldsmobile Division of GM, she received an MBA in marketing from the University of Michigan Ross School of Business, where she was the president of the Student Council. After completing her MBA, she was an executive in both marketing and sales for Johnson Controls' Plastic Container Division, where she was the first female and youngest national account manager for the $75 million PepsiCo account. She earned her Ph.D. in Marketing Communications from the University of North Carolina at Chapel Hill.

Dr. Aneil Mishra

Dr. Aneil Mishra is the Dean of the School of Management at the University of Michigan-Flint. He is an internationally recognized and widely published thought leader, educator, and consultant in the areas of trust, leadership, change management, organizational culture, and healthcare innovation. Aneil consults with a variety of start-ups, Fortune 100 firms, healthcare organizations, and nonprofits around the globe on strategy and innovation development, leadership/team development, and building trust-based cultures. He has been a faculty member of the Wharton School's American Bankers Association (ABA) Stonier Graduate School of Banking since 2017, and a finals judge for the Entrepreneurs' Organization's Global Student Entrepreneur Awards since 2016. He also serves on the board of Visionwalk Ministries of Dallas, Texas.

Aneil is also the co-author of four books: *Becoming a Trustworthy Leader: Psychology and Practice* (2013; 2021, Routledge), *College to Career: Your Guide to Getting Your Dream Job* (2020), *Trust Is Everything: Become the Leader Others Will Follow* (2008). Aneil is also the editor of the book *Restoring Trust in Higher Education: Making the Investment Worthwhile Again* (2017). Aneil publishes his research in many leading management, health care, and medical journals, with over 15,000 Google Scholar citations. He has served as an associate editor or editorial board member of several research journals, and currently is on the board of the *Journal of Applied Behavior Science*. His work is regularly profiled by leading news outlets.

From 2014 through 2021, Aneil was the Thomas D. Arthur Distinguished Professor of Leadership at the College of Business at East Carolina University. Before that, he was Associate Dean for Academic Affairs at North Carolina Central University, and VP of Curriculum and Faculty Relations for 2U Inc., where he helped to successfully develop and launch UNC-Chapel Hill's Kenan-Flagler School of Business's online MBA program, MBA@UNC. Aneil has also been an award-winning faculty member at Wake Forest, Duke, Penn State, and Michigan State. Aneil earned his A.B. in Economics, *cum laude*, from Princeton University. Prior to earning his Ph.D., Aneil worked for GM as a human resource specialist and manufacturing engineer. Aneil is a member of the Academy of Management, the International Leadership Association, and the Management and Organizational Behavior Teaching Society. He has also served as a management professor at Wake Forest, Michigan State, and Penn State.

Ted Castle
Owner and President, Rhino Foods

Rhino Foods has spent 40 years working to live up to our purpose: *Impacting the manner in which business is done.* I believe every business owner has a passion that is a source of great motivation. Mine is about finding ways to create positive social change through business. As a privately held business, we emphasize long-term financial health in order to invest in our customers, employees, and community. I have developed a love of business because it keeps me on my toes addressing the daily challenges of reducing risks and leveraging opportunities. I enjoy my work and the journey that I (along with fellow Rhino employees) have traveled since founding the business with my wife Anne in 1981.

As a relatively small company, our employees believe developing and making products for some of the largest food companies in the world, the right venue for our creative energies. I am very proud that we co-invented the number one ice cream flavor innovation in the last 30 years, we created the number two best-selling ice cream novelty in C-stores for a three-year period, and we developed the best-selling reduced-fat retail cheesecake for ten years. Though my passion keeps me deeply engaged at Rhino, my family has always come first in my life. I am fortunate that my wife, Anne, has been supportive of the time and efforts it takes to own and grow our business. Anne and I, along with our sons Ned and Rooney, have always enjoyed being active together in sports, travel, or at home. We are now "empty nesters" but still enjoy having our family nearby.

Chris Deshazor
Director, Talent and Org Development, Harness

Steve Fitzgerald
Chief Executive Officer of the Firestorm Group Ltd

Steve Fitzgerald is the Chief Executive Officer of the FireStorm Group Ltd, an eclectic collection of enterprises spanning human capital consulting, art, and real estate. He coaches C-Suite executives (with a special program for Chief HR Officers new to their role) and consults on the topic of talent management, specifically focused on the development of critical talent, executive succession, creativity, culture & change, M&A integration, and human capital strategy. He thrives when faced with the hard-to-solve people problem.

Steve's executive career spanned 30+ years, where he held the top HR Officer/Talent position at firms including Bridgewater Associates, Visteon, Vail Resorts, and Fairlane Credit. He also held executive roles at Silicon Valley outfits such as Sun Microsystems and Avaya, spending over a dozen years of his career in that sector. Steve credits his early years at Ford Motor Company (after coming out of graduate school at Michigan State) as being foundational in building early mental maps for the systematic development of talent in a 100+ year old enterprise. Learn more at www.FirestormGroup.net.

Outside of consulting, Steve splits his time between various ventures. He is a Senior Advisor to the impact-investing, private equity firm New Market Venture Partners. He serves on the Board of Cruxpoint, a firm focused on the identification and reversal of heart disease, and on the Board of the Colorado

Headwaters Land Trust, an organization dedicated to preserving the wild character and precious water of the land adjacent to Rocky Mountain National Park. He chairs the Fraser Public Arts Committee, is President of Fraser Valley Arts (501c3), and is the owner and principal artist of Firestorm Clayworks, an award-winning art pottery focused on hand-thrown, raku-fired pieces. You can see his artwork at www.FirestormClayworks.com.

For fun, Steve is quite active athletically, participating in cycling, Nordic, alpine, and backcountry skiing, fly fishing, hockey, and a variety of other outdoor pursuits as the seasons change. He and his wife Diana have been married for 30+ years and live in the Fraser Valley, Colorado, near Winter Park. Their adult sons Sean and Ryan live in Boulder, Colorado and Jackson, Wyoming, respectively.

Mike Gannon, Semi-Retired

Mike has more than 20 years of C-Suite experience at General Motors, Delphi, Nexteer, and the Johnson Electric Group. He has lived and worked in Asia, Europe and the USA, and held positions as SVP, COO, Product Line Executive, Commercial Officer and Chief Human Resource Officer. Mike earned his MBA from the University of Michigan and a BIA from Kettering University (formerly GMI). He is semi-retired and he and his wife Bonnie divide their time between Michigan and Florida. Mike loves spending time with his grandchildren, boating and when the weather is perfect, taking "Spartacus," his 1953 Chevy pick-up, for a drive.

Anita Riddle Johnson, Retired

Anita Riddle Johnson is a retired Executive of General Motors Company, Corporate Labor Staff. Her last leadership position was as Director, Labor Relations for the Customer Care and Aftersales Division for automotive parts processing and warehousing plants. Anita's background includes a number of key human resources and labor positions at the manufacturing operations, division and corporate levels of the company including Labor Director—Strategic Manpower & Employment, Personnel Director—Worldwide Facilities Group, Assistant HRM Director for North America Car Group, Corporate Sr. Classified Compensation Consultant and Manager - Strategic Human Resource Planning and Organizational Development. She was President for the GM African Ancestry Network employee resource group with previous responsibility as Executive Champion for the Employee Development Committee. Anita is a Michigan Chronicle Women of Excellence honoree, twice a GM Chairman's Honors award recipient, received the Chairman's Award for Excellence in Community Activities and is a member of Alpha Kappa Alpha Sorority, Inc. A native of Lansing, Michigan and current resident of Ann Arbor, Anita earned a Bachelor of Business Administration degree from the University of Michigan, is a former Regent's Alumni Scholar and holds a Master of Management degree from the J.L. Kellogg Graduate School of Management at Northwestern University.

Jeremy Kane
Managing Executive, Galapagos

Jeremy Kane is one of the founding partners of Galapagos Marketing. His focus is strategic marketing planning, with an emphasis on helping clients achieve competitive advantage, long-term growth, and adapting successfully to a changing marketplace. His career in financial services marketing extends 23 years and began with a leading Midwest branding agency. From there, he joined Crowe Horwath as a founding member of a new Financial Institutions sales and marketing practice, helping to grow the group from eight to 60 people in three years. He became the Partner-in-Charge of the practice in 2005.

During his career in Financial Services, Jeremy has worked with national, regional, community, de novo, and online-only institutions, preferring most to work with leadership teams of community-focused institutions. Prior to focusing on FIs, he gained significant experience in B2B marketing, managing accounts with Dow Chemical, Dow Corning, General Motors, and La-Z-Boy Furniture.

He earned his undergraduate degree from Reading University in England and his master's from Bowling Green State University in Ohio. Jeremy has a graduate degree in Bank Marketing from The University of Colorado. An avid soccer fan, Jeremy has played the game for over 50 years and coached it for 14. He enjoys the outdoors—and loves to hike, kayak, or bike out west. He's a community ambassador and head soccer coach for the YMCA and a volunteer soccer coach for a west Michigan-based Orphan Refugee charity organization.

Cem Kozlu
Former Chairman, Turkish Airlines; Chairman, Global Relations Forum

Kozlu has served as Chairman and CEO of Turkish Airlines in two periods between 1988 and 2003 for a total of 10 years. He has had other executive duties as the President of Komili Co. in Turkey and as the President of The Coca-Cola Company's Central Europe, Eurasia and Middle East Group. During 1991–1995, he was a member of the Turkish Parliament. He was Chairman of the Association of European Airlines in 1990. He is currently Chairman of Global Relations Forum and is a member of several corporate boards. He is the author of 10 books and producer of two TV series on leadership.

Bob Lintz
Trustee, The Cleveland Clinic
Former Plant Manager of the GM/Parma Plant

Anitra Manning
Americas D&I Strategy and Programs Leader, IBM

A strategic creative with a love for reimagining traditional human capital systems to meet the needs of an agile workplace, Dr. Anitra Manning is the Americas D&I Strategy and Programs Leader at IBM. In her role, she leads a team of diversity and inclusion professionals dedicated to providing strategic consulting, talent management, and programmatic support to technology and sales leaders. Anitra brings strong experience across nonprofit, academic, and financial services sectors to the service of corporate D&I and talent strategies.

Anitra holds a Doctor of Education in administrative and policy studies from the University of Pittsburgh where she was an Irvis Fellow. earned a Master of Science degree in public policy and management from Carnegie Mellon University's Heinz College where she was a H. John Heinz III Fellow for Service to Communities, Families, and Schools and research assistant. She is an extremely proud alumna of Hampton University where she earned a Bachelor of Arts in Political Science. Anitra holds coaching, assessment, change management, design thinking, project management, and talent certifications, supporting her in leveraging data to support leaders.

A native New Yorker, Anitra grew up savoring the smells of ethnic eateries; appreciating the sounds of jazz, gospel, and hip-hop emanating from cars, boom boxes, choir lofts, and outdoor concerts; embracing its vibrant arts scene; and feeling the nurture of her neighbors, educators, and pastors. She fiercely loves and most adores the titles daughter, sister, aunt, and friend and true to her New York childhood experience enjoys jazz and R&B concerts, the theater, travel, prayer, and meditative walking.

Jim McCown
Vice President at Tasco Sales Reps

Jim McCown has spent 30+ years in the Automotive Aftermarket working in Mexico, Canada and the United States.

Jenny Meyer
President & Ceo, Jem Advisors

Jenny Meyer spent eight years in the private equity trenches at SCF Partners, cultivating her experience through due diligence on several M&A transactions, IPOs and building the firm's business development process. Most recently, Jenny served as an executive and leadership team member of a boutique consulting firm, successfully developing strategy, and uncovering value for clients in industry. Jenny is now President & CEO of her own company, JEM Advisors, a recognized leader of value optimization in the energy, manufacturing, and petrochemical industries. Jenny's sense of intuition, creativity and intentionality drives positive momentum and facilitates strong, long-term client relationships. As a leader, Jenny believes in core values which promote communication, collaboration, and client service. Jenny earned her MBA from the University of St. Thomas in Houston, Texas in 2001. When not plotting JEM's next strategic move, Jenny enjoys running at Hermann Park and serving as a hope warrior against suicide, depression, and substance abuse. Jenny proudly serves on The Harris Center Foundation Board of Directors, the Advisory Board of the Moores School of Music Society and is an avid supporter of the Stephen F. Austin Rodeo Team.

R. Charles Moyer, Ph.D.
Professor of Finance at the College of Business at the University of Louisville

Charlie Moyer served as Dean of the College of Business at the University of Louisville from 2005 through 2013. He was Dean of the Babcock Graduate School of Management at Wake Forest University from 1996 to 2003. He is now Professor of Finance in the College of Business at the University of Louisville. He is *dean emeritus* from Wake Forest University. His teaching and research interests include Corporate Finance, Corporate Governance, Venture Investing, Business Valuation, and Cost of Capital. He is the author of four textbooks, including *Contemporary Financial Management* (14th edition, Cengage Publishing) and numerous articles appearing in leading finance and management journals. He has provided testimony in more than 80 public utility rate cases.

Charlie was a director at King Pharmaceuticals from 2000 until 2011, when King was acquired by Pfizer. He served on the Corporate Governance Committee, the Compensation Committee, the Risk Committee, and chaired the Audit Committee. He was a director of Kentucky Seed Capital Fund, and is a director of the Enterprise Angels Community Fund I, Summit Biosciences, USWorldMeds, and Capitala, a public BDC.

Dr. Moyer earned his Doctorate in Finance and Managerial Economics from the University of Pittsburgh in 1971, his Master of Business Administration from the University of Pittsburgh in 1968, and his Bachelor of Arts in Economics and German from Howard University in 1967.

Samantha Pittman
Talent Manager, Robert Half

Samantha works with senior level executives, decision-makers, and leadership teams to transform and strategize talent solutions by providing market data, workforce analysis, and performance updates to help them make effective hiring decisions.

Dennis Quaintance
CEO, CDO (Chief Design Officer) & CSO (Chief Storytelling Officer) Quaintance-Weaver Restaurants & Hotels

Dennis Quaintance announces that QW is now owned by QW staff members! November 17, 2016. In 1973, he began his hospitality career at age 15 as a housekeeper's assistant at a hotel in Missoula, Montana. He worked his way up to assistant general manager while in high school.

For four years after high school, he worked in leadership at several hotels around the Northwest, Arizona and Florida. In 1978, he moved to Greensboro, North Carolina, to help a friend open a restaurant, Franklin's Off Friendly. Dennis teamed up with Mike Weaver to form Quaintance-Weaver in 1988 and opened Lucky 32 restaurant in Greensboro in 1989. Lucky 32 was named for Dennis' father's racecar ('46 Mercury with a flathead V8). Today, the Quaintance-Weaver family of businesses includes a second Lucky 32

Southern Kitchen in Cary. The four-diamond, 130-room O. Henry Hotel and the adjacent Green Valley Grill opened in Greensboro in 1998. The four-diamond 147-room Proximity Hotel and neighboring Print Works Bistro opened in 2007 and are the first hotel and restaurant to gain Platinum certification with the US Green Building Council's Leadership in Energy and Environmental Design (LEED) program. Since 2014 QW also has the QW Craft Guild; a group of 10 to 16 full time and adjunct artists and craftspeople that make and restore items and spaces for the QW businesses. He married Nancy King in 1983. Nancy is VP of QW and focuses on hotel marketing and operations plus she is a member of the culinary team. She was an executive with two different hotel companies prior to joining QW. She started her career at age 15 with Disney and graduated with honors from Cornell University School of Hotel Administration.

Daniel Quinn
Member at Inception Micro Angel Fund (IMAF)-RTP

Daniel Quinn has held senior level positions in both the private and public sector and positions such as President, Director, and Chief Financial Officer. He has been a part of multiple successful start-ups and business acquisitions. He sits on the board of several company's and services as member and advisor for a private investment group and is also an Iraq and Afghanistan combat veteran.

John Rogers
Chairman, Co-CEO, & Chief Investment Officer, Ariel Investments

John's passion for investing began at age 12 when his father began buying him stocks as Christmas and birthday gifts. His interest in equities grew at Princeton University, where he majored in economics, and over the two-plus years he worked as a stockbroker for William Blair & Company, LLC. In 1983, John founded Ariel to focus on patient, value investing within small- and medium-sized companies. While our research capabilities have expanded across the globe, patience is still the disciplined approach that drives the firm today. Early in his career, John's investment acumen brought him to the forefront of media attention and culminated in him being selected as Co-Mutual Fund Manager of the Year by *Sylvia Porter's Personal Finance* magazine as well as an All-Star Mutual Fund Manager by *USA TODAY*. Furthermore, John has been highlighted alongside legendary investors Warren Buffett, Sir John Templeton and Ben Graham in the distinguished book: *The World's 99 Greatest Investors* by Magnus Angenfelt.

His professional accomplishments extend to the boardroom where he is a member of the board of directors of McDonald's, NIKE, The New York Times Company, and Ryan Specialty Group Holdings. John also serves as vice chair of the board of trustees of the University of Chicago. Additionally, he is a member of the American Academy of Arts and Sciences, and a director of the Robert F. Kennedy Center for Justice and Human Rights. In 2008, John was awarded Princeton University's highest honor, the Woodrow Wilson Award, presented each year to the alumnus or alumna whose career embodies a commitment to national service. Following the election of President Barack

Obama, John served as co-chair for the Presidential Inaugural Committee 2009, and more recently, he joined the Barack Obama Foundation's Board of Directors. John received an AB in economics from Princeton University, where he was also captain of the varsity basketball team.

Dr. Bruce Rubin, MEngr, MD, MBA, FAAP, FRCPC
Jessie Ball Dupont Distinguished Professor of Pediatrics at Children's Hospital of Richmond at VCU

Dr. Rubin served as Jesse Ball DuPont Distinguished Professor and Chair of the Department of Pediatrics from 2009 to 2020 and Physician in Chief of the Children's Hospital of Richmond at VCU from 2010 to 2020. He is also a Professor in the VCU College of Engineering and Adjunct Professor of Physiology and Biophysics. Dr. Rubin came to VCU after 12 years at Wake Forest University in Winston-Salem, N.C., where he was professor and vice chair for research in the pediatrics department. He has been named a Virginia Eminent Scholar in Pediatrics.

Dr. Rubin received his undergraduate Bachelor of Science in math and physics, Master of Engineering and Medical degrees from Tulane University in New Orleans. He is a Rhodes Scholar, and conducted postdoctoral work in biomedical engineering at Oxford University. He also earned an MBA at Wake Forest University. He is a member of Board of the Virginia March of Dimes, The Virginia Board of Health Professions, the VCU Center for Communication and Health, the International Congress of Pediatric Pulmonology (CIPP), and the American Respiratory Care Foundation, and he is Medical Advisor to the Virginia Society of Respiratory Care. He is a fellow of the American Academy of Pediatrics and of the Royal College of Physicians and Surgeons of Canada.

Dr. Rubin received the Forest Bird Lifetime Scientific Achievement Award as well as the Jimmy A. Young Medal from the AARC, the Prix extraordinaire from CIPP and he is a Prix Galien Laurate. He holds honorary appointments in four medical schools, is on the editorial board of 11 journals, has published more than 300 original research papers and chapters, and holds 10 patents. His research focus is regulation of mucus clearance in health and disease, airway inflammation and immunomodulation, cough, and aerosol delivery of medications.

Dr. Rubin is also a magician, elected to membership in the International Brotherhood of Magicians (Wizard Award) and over the past 25 years has taught medical magic in 40 countries on 5 continents.

Juan Carlos Sanchez
GM/Business Leader, Smarter
Successful and charismatic executive with 25+ years of experience in both small companies and the Fortune 10. Well-rounded background in Telecom, Tech, Finance, Engineering, and Construction. Led complex global programs across multiple countries (Americas, Asia, Europe) ranging from $15M to multibillion dollar operations. Proven track record in delivering customer-centric solutions in B2B and B2C environments.

Kellie Sauls
Director of Diversity, Equity, & Inclusion for the Teacher Retirement System of Texas

Kellie Sauls serves as the Director of Diversity, Equity, & Inclusion for the Teacher Retirement System of Texas where she is responsible for the direction and oversight of DE&I strategy, planning, program development, and management across the organization. Prior to TRS, Kellie spent over 20 years in higher education primarily in graduate business programs at the University of Texas, University of Virginia, and Wake Forest University. Kellie recently completed Leadership Austin and was elected by her class to represent them on the Board of Directors. In addition to her impactful volunteer work within the community, she co-founded a TEDx program in Charlottesville, Virginia, has provided DE&I consultation services, and has served on several local and national diversity related advisory councils.

Brent Senior, M.D.
UNC-Chapel School of Medicine. Vice Chair of Academics and Outreach; Nathaniel and Sheila Harris Distinguished Professor; Chief, Division of Rhinology, Allergy, and Endoscopic Skull Base Surgery.

Brent A. Senior, MD, FACS, FARS is Nat and Sheila Harris Distinguished Professor of Otolaryngology and Neurosurgery at the University of North Carolina at Chapel Hill where he also serves as Vice Chair of Academic Affairs and Outreach and Chief of Rhinology, Allergy, and Endoscopic Skull Base Surgery. Dr. Senior has lectured and instructed in nearly 120 national and international rhinology courses and authored 120 articles and chapters in the field. In addition, he has co-edited three texts in rhinology including the "The Frontal Sinus," now in its second edition, and recently, the "Rhinology and Allergy Clinical Reference Guide." Dr. Senior's passion for education has been honored with his receipt of "Teacher of the Year" awards and the "Golden Head Mirror Award" from the American Rhinologic Society, while his clinical expertise has been honored with several "Top Doctor" awards. His humanitarian efforts garnered him a "Humanitarian of the Year" Award from the American Academy of Otolaryngology in 2005. He is immediate past-Chair of Rhinology and Allergy Education for the American Academy of Otolaryngology/Head and Neck Surgery; Associate Editor of the International Forum of Allergy and Rhinology; Past President of the American Rhinologic Society; President of the Christian Society of Otolaryngology; and he sits on the Board of Directors of the International Rhinologic Society and the American Academy of Otolaryngology/Head and Neck Surgery. He is also President of the International Rhinologic Society.

Hal Stern
VP & CIO, Janssen R&D

Hal Stern is the VP and CIO of Janssen R&D, where his team designs and delivers end to end systems to support discovery, early development, clinical development, regulatory, safety, and quality processes. Hal has strong interests in data science, non-traditional and applied computing techniques, security, privacy, large-scale networking, and intellectual property management and policies. Hal joined Janssen from Merck & Company, where he was AVP, Merck Research Labs Engineering. Before joining Merck, Hal had a 25-year career in the technology industry, with variety of software and services leadership positions at Juniper Networks, Oracle Corporation, and Sun Microsystems.

He is co-inventor on 11 United States patents in the areas of networking, security and user experience and co-author of three technical books. Hal holds a BSE in Electrical Engineering and Computer Science from Princeton University, and he serves on the graduate board of the Colonial Club at Princeton and the advisory board of Sympatic. Hal and his wife Toby have two adult children, and outside of work he plays the bass guitar, coaches Under-8 Mite ice hockey for the New Jersey Devils Youth club, and enjoys live music, photography, cooking, reading, and travel.

Larry Stimpert, Ph.D.
President, Hampden-Sydney College

Larry Stimpert is the 25th president of Hampden-Sydney College. Before coming to Hampden-Sydney, Dr. Stimpert served as Vice President for Academic Affairs and Professor of Economics and Management at DePauw University. Earlier, he served as a professor in the Economics and Business Department at Colorado College and held the John L. Knight Chair for the Study of Free Enterprise.

Dr. Stimpert received his B.A. in economics, *magna cum laude*, from Illinois Wesleyan University, his M.B.A. from Columbia University, and his Ph.D. from the University of Illinois at Urbana-Champaign. His scholarship focuses on top managers and their influence on strategic decision making and firm strategies. His articles on a variety of management topics have appeared in leading academic journals, and he is the co-author of two management textbooks.

Before starting his academic career, Dr. Stimpert worked for the Norfolk Southern Corporation and the Chicago and North Western Transportation Company. Dr. Stimpert and his wife, Lesley, have two children.

Tom Tymann
Project Specialist, Lowes Home Improvement

Tom is responsible for sales of exterior projects at Lowes that include Windows, Siding, Decking, Fencing, Roofing, Gutters, and HVAC. In 2018, Tom became the 1st project specialist in Charlotte market to exceed $2 million in sales volume, generating over $500k in referral business. In 2014, Tom was first project specialist in market to exceed $1 million in sales volume at $1.3 million. From 2014 to 2018, Tom ranked in the top 10 of sales specialists in the company (out of 1700+).

Pastor Jim Wenger
St. John Lutheran Church in Deshler, Ohio

He is an ordained Lutheran pastor of the Evangelical Lutheran Church in America. He received his bachelor's degree from Wartburg College in Waverly, Iowa, and his master's of divinity from Wartburg Seminar in Dubuque, Iowa. He is the son and grandson of Lutheran pastors, but most importantly, he is a servant of the most high God, who is most clearly known in the person of Jesus of Nazareth, by the power of the Holy Spirit.

Joe Wilcox
Foreign Service Specialist, U.S. Department of State

Joseph Wilcox is an American diplomat in the United States Foreign Service working as a Facilities Manager (FM). Joseph is currently serving overseas in Hermosillo, Mexico as the FM at the US Consulate, and assisting with the development and construction of the new US Consulate, valued over $200M. Prior to working for the Foreign Service, Joseph was a FM for the US Air Force in South Korea. Additionally, Joseph spent 8 years active duty in the US Marine Corps where he obtained the rank of Sergeant and had multiple combat deployments to Afghanistan, as well as leading international teams globally in Japan, Morocco, Thailand, and Afghanistan. Joseph earned his Master's in Business Administration from North Carolina State University, and his Bachelor's in Legal Studies from the University of Maryland University College.

Phil Wilhelm
GM of SMB Sales, Fortinet

Phil Wilhelm is the GM of SMB Sales for Fortinet. After 13+ years of sales and executive leadership roles with value-added resellers, Phil joined Fortinet in 2019 to build out the team and capabilities for this fast-growing segment of the market. Phil graduated from the University of Texas and resides in Austin, TX with his wife, children and two corgis. In his spare time Phil analyzes the parallels between the Grateful Dead and organizational leadership.

Brooke Wilson
Two Men and a Truck, International

Brooke Wilson is the multi-unit franchise owner of Two Men and a Truck, International, and president of Lead Dog Ventures. She owns 5 Two Men and a Truck units with her husband and business partner, Les Wilson. They live in NC with their three dogs and one cat. The moving business has been good to Brooke Wilson and her husband and business partner Les. Together the couple has built a company with multiple Two Men and a Truck territories that generate annual revenue of more than $12 million. Today, the couple controls the Raleigh-Durham Research Triangle market and the South Atlanta market with five franchise operations across the two states.

APPENDIX 2: BACKGROUND ON THE RESEARCH FOR THIS BOOK

We originally learned how essential it is to have a culture of trust in the context of a crisis. As part of his dissertation, Aneil studied how the North American automotive industry was undergoing significant upheaval in the 1980s and early 1990s based on its unwillingness to deal with Japanese competitors, who had been rapidly growing their share of the North American car and truck market beginning in the early 1970s. In failing to develop their own fuel-efficient and highly reliable cars, the Big Three (GM, Ford, and Chrysler) had laid off tens of thousands of their employees and permanently shut down dozens of assembly and other manufacturing plants during this time. Not surprisingly, they had also destroyed whatever trust they had built with their employees, most of whom would never again earn the incomes that had moved millions of people into the middle class beginning in the 1950s.

In this context, Aneil had identified a GM plant that had been a noticeable, positive outlier in a sample of 22 GM plants and eight of their suppliers that a University of Michigan School of Business study had identified in 1989.[1] Bob Lintz's organization, GM Parma Metal Fabrication Plant, reported some of the highest levels of employee trust in the plant's top management, and Bob's interviews revealed a very different manager to the typical ones Aneil and Karen had worked for in their GM careers or that Aneil had been interviewing as part of his research. In particular, Bob talked about the significant effort he and his management team had made to build a collaborative working relationship with the local UAW chapter, as well as across operations throughout the plant. As we've continued our relationship with Bob, we decided to write about him books so that we could share his leadership wisdom with a new generation of leaders.

TRUST SURVEY

TRUST

(1) Management is straightforward with me (open) 1 2 3 4 5

(2) Management is competent and knowledgeable (competent) 1 2 3 4 5

(3) Management does not try to get out of its commitments (reliable) 1 2 3 4 5

(4) Management does not take advantage of me (compassion) 1 2 3 4 5

(5) Management communicates honestly with me (open) 1 2 3 4 5

(6) Management can contribute to my organization's success (competent) 1 2 3 4 5

(7) Management behaves consistently (reliable) 1 2 3 4 5

(8) Management does not exploit me (compassion) 1 2 3 4 5

(9) Management does not mislead me in their communications (open) 1 2 3 4 5

(10) Management can help my organization survive during the next

decade (competent) 1 2 3 4 5

(11) Management is reliable (reliable) 1 2 3 4 5

(12) Management cares about my best interests (compassion) 1 2 3 4 5

(13) Management does not withhold important information from me (open) 1 2 3 4 5

(14) Management is concerned for my welfare (compassion) 1 2 3 4 5

(15) Management can be counted on (reliable) 1 2 3 4 5

(16) Management can help solve important problems faced by

my organization (competent) 1 2 3 4 5

(17) Management can be trusted (trust) 1 2 3 4 5

This instrument (in its current form or in previous versions) was originally published in:

Mishra, Aneil K. and Mishra, Karen E. (1994). The role of mutual trust in effective downsizing strategies, *Human Resource Management*, 33 (2), 261-279.

Source: Copyright [Mishra & Mishra 1994]. Reproduced with permission.

Note

1. As part of this study, employees in each organization were surveyed every six months on a number of topics, including their attitudes toward management, work practices, and organizational culture.

INDEX

Note: *Italicised* page numbers refer to figures and **bold** page numbers refer to tables in the text.

For Product Safety Concerns and Information please contact our EU
representative GPSR@taylorandfrancis.com
Taylor & Francis Verlag GmbH, Kaufingerstraße 24, 80331 München, Germany

www.ingramcontent.com/pod-product-compliance
Ingram Content Group UK Ltd.
Pitfield, Milton Keynes, MK11 3LW, UK
UKHW021447080625
459435UK00012B/399

* 9 7 8 0 3 6 7 4 2 1 4 5 8 *